D1542761

Read On . . . Biography

Recent Titles in Libraries Unlimited Read On Series
Barry Trott, Series Editor

Read On . . . Historical Fiction: Reading Lists for Every Taste
Brad Hooper

Read On . . . Horror Fiction: Reading Lists for Every Taste
June Michele Pulliam and Anthony J. Fonseca

Read On . . . Fantasy Fiction: Reading Lists for Every Taste
Neil Hollands

Read On . . . Crime Fiction: Reading Lists for Every Taste
Barry Trott

Read On . . . Women's Fiction: Reading Lists for Every Taste
Rebecca Vnuk

Read On . . . Life Stories: Reading Lists for Every Taste
Rosalind Reisner

Read On . . . Science Fiction: Reading Lists for Every Taste
Steven A. Torres-Roman

Read On . . . Audiobooks: Reading Lists for Every Taste
Joyce G. Saricks

Read On . . . Graphic Novels: Reading Lists for Every Taste
Abby Alpert

Read On . . . Biography

Reading Lists for Every Taste

Rick Roche

Read On Series
Barry Trott, Series Editor

LIBRARIES UNLIMITED

AN IMPRINT OF ABC-CLIO, LLC
Santa Barbara, California • Denver, Colorado • Oxford, England

Library of Congress Cataloging-in-Publication Data

Roche, Rick.
  Read on— biography : reading lists for every taste / Rick Roche.
     p. cm. — (Read on series)
  Includes index.
  ISBN 978-1-59884-701-7 (hardcopy : alk. paper) — ISBN 978-1-61069-179-6 (ebook) 1. Biography—Bibliography. 2. Autobiography—Bibliography.
I. Title.
  Z5301.R558   2012
  [CT104]
  016.92—dc23   2011046293

ISBN: 978-1-59884-701-7
EISBN: 978-1-61069-179-6

16   15   14   13   12   1   2   3   4   5

This book is also available on the World Wide Web as an eBook.
Visit www.abc-clio.com for details.

Libraries Unlimited
An Imprint of ABC-CLIO, LLC

ABC-CLIO, LLC
130 Cremona Drive, P.O. Box 1911
Santa Barbara, California 93116-1911

This book is printed on acid-free paper ∞

Manufactured in the United States of America

Contents

Series Foreword

Welcome to Libraries Unlimited's Read On series of fiction and nonfiction genre guides for readers' advisors and for readers. The Read On series introduces readers and those who work with them to new ways of looking at books, genres, and reading interests.

Over the past decade, readers' advisory services have become vital in public libraries. A quick glance at the schedule of any library conference at the state or national level will reveal a wealth of programs on various aspects of connecting readers to books they will enjoy. Working with unfamiliar genres or types of reading can be a challenge, particularly for those new to the field. Equally, readers may find it a bit overwhelming to look for books outside their favorite authors and preferred reading interests. The titles in the Read On series offer you a new way to approach reading:

- they introduce you to a broad sampling of materials available in a given genre;
- they offer you new directions to explore in a genre—through appeal features and unconventional topics;
- they help readers' advisors better understand and navigate genres with which they are less familiar; and
- they provide reading lists that you can use to create quick displays, include on your library websites and in the library newsletter, or hand out to readers.

The lists in the Read On series are arranged in sections based on appeal characteristics—story, character, setting, and language (as described in Joyce Saricks's *Reader's Advisory Services in the Public Library*, 3d ed., ALA Editions, 2005), with a fifth section on mood. These are hidden elements of a book that attract readers. Remember that a book can have multiple appeal factors; and sometimes readers are drawn to a particular book for several factors, while other times for only one. In the Read On lists, titles are placed according to their primary appeal characteristics and then put into a list that reflects common reading interests. So, if you are working with a reader who loves fantasy that features quests for magical objects or a reader who is interested in memoirs with a strong sense of place, you will be able to find a list of titles whose main appeal centers around this search. Each list indicates a title that is an especially good starting place for readers, an exemplar of that appeal characteristic.

Story is perhaps the most basic appeal characteristic. It relates to the plot of the book—what are the elements of the tale? Is the emphasis more on the people or the situations? Is the story action focused or more interior? Is it funny? Scary?

Many readers are drawn to the books they love by the characters. The character appeal reflects such aspects as whether there are lots of characters or only a single main character; Are the characters easily recognizable types? Do the characters grow and change over the course of the story? What are the characters' occupations?

Setting covers a range of elements that might appeal to readers. What is the time period or geographic locale of the tale? How much does the author describe the surroundings of the story? Does the reader feel as though he or she is there, when reading the book? Are there special features such as the monastic location of Ellis Peters's Brother Cadfael mysteries or the small-town setting of Jan Karon's Mitford series?

Although not traditionally considered appeal characteristic, mood is important to readers as well. It relates to how the author uses the tools of narrative—language, pacing, story, and character—to create a feeling for the work. Mood can be difficult to quantify because the reader brings his or her own feelings to the story as well. Mood really asks how does the book make the reader feel: Creepy? Refreshed? Joyful? Sad?

Finally, the language appeal brings together titles where the author's writing style draws the reader. This can be anything from a lyrical prose style with lots of flourishes to a spare use of language à la Hemingway. Humor, snappy dialog, wordplay, recipes, and other language elements all have the potential to attract readers.

Dig into these lists. Use them to find new titles and authors in a genre that you love, or as a guide to expand your knowledge of a new type of writing . . . Above all, read, enjoy, and remember—never apologize for your reading tastes!

Barry Trott
Series Editor

Acknowledgments

Thanks to my wife, Bonnie Reid, who loves correct punctuation and finding the right words. Her knowledge of historical figures has also been helpful. Her relief that the book is completed is as great as mine.

Thanks to my editors, Barry Trott and Barbara Ittner, who gave me the chance to write this book and helped with the organization of lists by appeal factors. Their help was essential.

Thanks again to the selectors at the Thomas Ford Memorial Library and Downers Grove Public Library who stocked their shelves with great books and to the circulation staffs who loaned many of them to me. The books that I reviewed passed through many hands.

Thanks to all the authors who have spent years researching and writing about the lives of remarkable people. They have enlightened and entertained me with their wonderful stories.

Finally, thanks to all the readers who come to the library and ask for something good to read. I have enjoyed our conversations and love seeing them leave with books. Keep coming.

Introduction

When a president leaves office, a great athlete retires, or a popular movie star dies, biographies begin to appear in bookstores and on library shelves. Biographers know that there are readers eager to learn more about eminent people once their work or lives have ended. Followers long to have questions answered, details verified, and lives assessed. For the most important political figures, monarchs, military leaders, notorious criminals, and celebrated cultural icons, their lives in books may be just beginning. We are still reading about Socrates, Cleopatra, Michelangelo, William Shakespeare, George Washington, Jesse James, and Albert Einstein many years after their deaths.

Evidence of biography's popularity is easy to find. As I write in April 2011, *Unbroken: A World War II Story of Survival, Resilience, and Redemption* by Laura Hillenbrand has been on the *New York Times* hardcover nonfiction best-seller list for 20 weeks. This book about Lieutenant Louis Zamperini, a former Olympic runner who was a prisoner of war, is number two on the list this week after being number one for many weeks. With it on the 15-book list are *Jesus of Nazareth* by Pope Joseph Ratzinger (4 weeks) and *Cleopatra: A Life* by Stacy Schiff (22 weeks). *Great Soul: Mahatma Gandhi and His Struggles with India* by Joseph Lelyveld was on the list last week. Zamperini is still living, but the other three are long dead and have been the subjects of many previous books.[1]

Biography has been a highly respected genre in critical circles for a long time. The Pulitzer Prize Board established an annual biography prize in 1917, which has since been joined by the *Los Angeles Times* Book Prize in 1980 and the National Book Critics Circle Award for Biography in 1983. The ALA Notable Books for Adults list has never been without a biography since its debut in 1944.[2] Most book review journals devote at least a small section to biography in every issue. There are always worthy new titles for devoted biography readers.

With so many biographies being published and acquired by libraries, readers sometimes struggle to find titles that appeal to them among the many library shelves devoted to the genre. The aim of this guide is to help these readers and the librarians who advise them to navigate the maze to find biographies that appeal to their love of character, story, setting, language, or mood. It is fitting that character is first mentioned as it is the primary appeal factor. Every biography has a clearly defined central character or group of characters around whom the action revolves. Discovering the motivations of these characters is a primary reason for writing and reading the books, but there is more to most great biographical writing. Readers find great stories, discover familiar or unfamiliar settings, enjoy stylish writing, and experience moods, as they would in any narrative literature. The book lists in this guide, organized by appeal factors, will help connect readers with biographies they will enjoy.

Biography Defined

What do we mean by biography? In an article in the *New Dictionary of the History of Ideas*, Frederic Liers explains that our English word was formed from the Greek roots *bios* (life) and *graphein* (writing). The word was not, however, used in English until 1683, when British author John Dryden wrote an introduction to a new translation of *Plutarch's Lives*. By biography Dryden meant a written account of the life of a person or persons who lived and could be identified.[3] Broadly used, the term may refer to any type of true life story, including first person accounts. For the sake of this guide, however, biography only refers to third-person accounts of others' lives. For memoirs and autobiographies, please turn to *Read On . . . Life Stories* by Rosalind Reisner (2009).

Dual biography refers to a book that tells the life stories of two individuals, whose lives may or may not have been linked. Married couples, brothers, business rivals, and friends are just a few of the relationships that have been considered in dual biographies.

Family biography refers to a book that focuses on two or more generations of related people. Families prominent in business, government, or the arts have been the subjects of family biographies.

Collective biography refers to a book that gathers several short biographies into one volume. The individuals profiled in a collective biography usually share traits, experiences, or occupations.

A Short History of the Motivation to Read Biography

The appeal of biography has broadened through history so that there are now many reasons to read the stories of famous people. Drawn from my "Chronology of Biographical History" in *Real Lives Revealed: A Guide to Reading Interests in Biography*, here are highlights in the development of biographical appeal.[4]

The earliest known examples of biography are funeral elegies written by Greeks in the 10th century BCE. These pieces that praised the departed must have been some comfort to both the writers and the readers who wished to remember their lost friends and family.

In the fifth century BCE, Greek poet Ion of Chios wrote tributes to states-man Pericles and playwright Sophocles. These commemorative pieces of lead-ers fostered pride among Greek followers who saw themselves together as part of a great society.

In his *Apology* and *Phaedo*, fourth-century BCE Greek philosopher Plato expanded the role of the tribute by writing in depth about his former teacher Socrates. Because Socrates had not recorded his teachings, they were in danger of being forgotten. By recounting Socrates's words and their meanings, Plato went far beyond just listing the facts and events in his mentor's life. Readers continue to seek these philosophically instructive pieces.

In the first century CE, Gospel writers Matthew, Mark, Luke, and John wrote about Jesus of Nazareth. They repeated his sermons and parables as well as reported his sacrificial death so that his followers might be guided in their faith. Christians still read their Gospels for instruction and inspiration.

In the second century, Greek author Plutarch wrote profiles of 46 Greek and Roman public figures. His *Parallel Lives* gave readers an opportunity to judge the moral characters of men who had shaped and ruled their societies.

In the seventh century, Irish abbot Adomnán of Iona wrote *Life of St. Columbae* in support of the canonization of the saint. According to many his-tories of biography, hagiographic writing that intended to support the faith of readers dominated European biography for a thousand years.

In 1771, Benjamin Franklin published his *Autobiography*, the first of many first-person and third-person accounts of self-made men. Throughout the late 18th and much of the 19th centuries, these books were popular with American readers wanting exemplary lives to emulate.

In 1791, James Boswell published *Life of Samuel Johnson*, a sympathetic account in which the author incorporated quotes from Johnson's letters and his own diaries, acquainting readers with intimate details of his friend's daily life.

In 1901, Charles L. C. Minor wrote *The Real Lincoln*, arguing that the mar-tyred president was a hypocrite and unscrupulous opportunist. This political biography appealed to readers with Confederate sympathies.

In 1918, Lytton Strachey published *Eminent Victorians* with its unflattering profiles of prominent British figures. It is generally considered the first of many 20th-century celebrity biographies to appeal to a reader's love of scandal.

In 1932, the Bobbs-Merrill Company began its *Childhood of Famous Americans* series, biographies for young readers that portrayed famous people as lively and curious children with whom they could easily identify. The series fostered reading biography from an early age.

In 1999, Lipper/Viking launched the *Penguin Lives* series with *Crazy Horse* by Larry McMurtry. These concise biographies from eminent novelists, histori-ans, and essayists offered readers strong character development and compelling stories without ponderous detail.

Criteria for Selection

The first consideration in selecting biographies for this guide was whether their subjects were likely to appeal to the general reading public. Many famous people from history and current events easily passed this test, and they were joined by selected lesser-known figures that lived unusual lives. To narrow the selections, the following criteria were also considered:

> Readability—Each book has an engaging narrative style. Books that seemed dry or academic were eliminated.
>
> Attractiveness of the physical books—Readable fonts and ample line spacing are as important in attracting readers as book jacket design. It is true that many readers choose a book by its cover, as well as size and overall appearance.
>
> Recent publishing dates—More than half of the 456 titles included in this guide were published between 2006 and 2010. Many should still be in print.
>
> Availability—All of the titles included in this guide were published in the United States and are readily available in public libraries. Most have 500 or more copies cited in the *WorldCat* database from OCLC, making them easy to interlibrary loan.

How to Use This Book

Like other titles in the Read On series, this guide is divided into five chapters based on reading appeal factors. Befitting biography as a genre, the first chapter focuses on character, the most obvious appeal element for books about the lives of people. Chapters focusing on story, setting, language, and mood follow.

Within each chapter are 8 to 15 annotated lists, each identifying 7 to 9 titles that share an appeal factor. Readers with particular character types or storylines in mind may use these lists to find suggested titles. For example, a reader who enjoys books about people who went out of their way to break societal conventions may turn to the character list "Eccentric Egos," where they will find biographies of artist Salvador Dalí, musician Frank Zappa, and author Mark Twain. Readers who admire people who worked their way out of poverty may appreciate books from the story list "Rags to Riches," which includes books about Thomas Lipton, the grocer who put loose tea into convenient bags, and A. G. Gaston, the black coal miner who turned income earned from selling lunches to other miners into a banking and insurance empire. Likewise, a reader seeking gentle reads may enjoy titles from the mood list "Heartwarming Stories," with books about priest Michael McGivney and flag maker Betsy Ross.

Readers may also discover titles to read through use of the index, which include authors, titles, and subjects.

Symbols Used in Annotations

▶ This title is a good first choice from its list.
≋ Book groups may enjoy this title.
♉ This book was given one or more of the following awards:

- American Library Association Notable Book
- Los Angeles Times Book Prize for Biography
- National Book Award for Nonfiction
- National Book Critics Circle Award for Biography
- Pulitzer Prize for Biography or Autobiography

Notes

1. "Hardcover Nonfiction," *New York Times Book Review,* April 17, 2011, 22.
2. Rick Roche, "Appendix A: Biography Awards," in *Real Lives Revealed: A Guide to Reading Interests in Biography* (Libraries Unlimited, 2009), 435–58.
3. Frederic Liers, "Biography," in *The New Dictionary of the History of Ideas,* ed. Maryanne Cline Horowitz (Charles Scribner's Sons, 2005), 1:217–20.
4. Rick Roche, "Chronology of Biographical History," in *Real Lives Revealed: A Guide to Reading Interests in Biography* (Libraries Unlimited, 2009), xxvii–xxxi.

Further Reading

Adamson, Lynda G. *Thematic Guide to Popular Nonfiction.* Greenwood Press, 2006.

Altick, Richard D. *Lives and Letters: A History of Literary Biography in England and America.* Alfred A. Knopf, 1996.

Burt, Daniel S. *The Biography Book: A Reader's Guide to Nonfiction, Fictional, and Film Biographies of More Than 500 of the Most Fascinating Individuals of All Time.* Oryx Press, 2001.

Casper, Scott. "Biography." In *American History through Literature 1820–1870.* Ed. Janet Gabler-Hover and Robert Sattelmeyer, vol. 1, 116–21. Charles Scribner's Sons, 2006.

Cords, Sarah. *The Real Story: A Guide to Nonfiction Reading Interests.* Libraries Unlimited, 2006.

Garrity, John. *The Nature of Biography.* Alfred A. Knopf, 1957.

Gittings, Robert. *The Nature of Biography.* University of Washington Press, 1977.

Hamilton, Nigel. *Biography: A Brief History.* Harvard University Press, 2007.

Hamilton, Nigel. *How to Do Biography: A Primer.* Harvard University Press, 2008.

Kenndall, Paul Murray. *The Art of Biography*. W. W. Norton, 1965.

Nicolson, Harold. *The Development of English Biography*. Harcourt, Brace and Company, 1928.

Novarr, David. *The Lines of Life: Theories of Biography, 1880–1970*. Purdue University Press, 1986.

Pannapacker, William. "Biography." In *American History Through Literature 1870–1920*. Ed. Tom Quirk and Gary Scharnhorst, vol. 1, 150–58. Charles Scribner's Sons, 2006.

Roche, Rick. *Real Lives Revealed: A Guide to Reading Interests in Biography*. Libraries Unlimited, 2009.

Rollyson, Carl. *Biography: A User's Guide*. Ivan R. Dee, 2008.

Whittemore, Reed. *Pure Lives: The Early Biographers*. Johns Hopkins University Press, 1988.

Whittemore, Reed. *Whole Lives: Shapers of Modern Biography*. Johns Hopkins University Press, 1989.

Wyatt, Neal. *The Reader's Advisory Guide to Nonfiction*. American Library Association, 2007.

Chapter One

Character

It may seem obvious. We read biographies to learn about other people's lives, especially wanting any riddles about their characters solved. What types of individuals were the famous people about whom we read? What compelled them to be who they were and do what they did? How were they different from us? Should we admire or condemn them? Biographers try to either answer these questions or provide ample evidence for us to reach our own conclusions.

To the chagrin of the cataloger of character types but to the pleasure of many readers, the character of famous people is often complex and difficult to label. For example, what kind of person was singer Johnny Cash? He abandoned his family, took drugs, and was obsessed with being a star. He could be judged irresponsible at best, yet he was adored by many fans that identified with his songs and forgave his failures. Like Cash, Confederate president Jefferson Davis and abolitionist John Brown are viewed as heroes or villains by different readers, and even biographers disagree. Heated debates about the characters of important public figures, such as John F. Kennedy or Ronald Reagan, result in a multitude of biographies, a rich collection of books that readers may enjoy.

In this chapter are 11 book lists featuring biographies of people with similar character types. I chose to start with "Determined Leaders" because I wanted a positive beginning for the chapter, a book list about people to admire—at least in the viewpoint of the biographer. Quickly look at the titles in this list and you may notice names that you might not expect, including Vietnamese leader Ho Chi Minh and Joanna I, Queen of Naples, Jerusalem, and Sicily. The first is remembered as America's enemy in the Vietnam War, while the second is mostly unknown to modern readers. In challenging our preconceptions and our

1

ignorance, their biographers complement and expand the literature about leadership, and we have more good books to read.

The characters in some of the subsequent lists are not to be admired, but the choices are meant to be enjoyed.

Determined Leaders

Military and political leaders, such as Andrew Jackson and Winston Churchill, inspired their followers to support them in times of war, natural disaster, economic trial, or political strife. Through words and actions, they stirred supporters to give more and risk more, even when the odds were poor. They often succeeded when they should not have, and their acts altered the course of history. The subjects in this list of dramatic biographies demonstrated such character.

Burstein, Andrew
The Passions of Andrew Jackson. 2003. Knopf. 292p. ISBN 0375414282. ☙

In frontier Tennessee, where he served as prosecutor, state judge, congressman, and senator, Andrew Jackson learned to gain and wield power. Thus empowered, he became a general without any significant military experience and nationally famous as the commander at the Battle of New Orleans in 1815. In this reassessment of the character of the man who became the seventh U.S. president, historian Andrew Burstein focuses on the alliances of a man full of contradictory notions. Both loved and hated, he was a divisive figure who strove to make his country a proud and independent military giant.

Duiker, William J.
Ho Chi Minh: A Life. 2000. Hyperion. 695p. ISBN 0786863870.

To most Americans, North Vietnamese leader Ho Chi Minh (1890–1969) was just an enemy about whom little was known. He had used various aliases in his career as a scholar, journalist, and revolutionary, and his role in the North Vietnamese government was misunderstood by Western analysts. Drawing on his years of reading once-classified Foreign Service reports, historian William J. Duiker reveals in this extensive but easy-to-read book that the Communist leader was both an astute politician and a revered symbol for a small nation that outlasted its French and American opponents.

Ellis, Joseph J.
▶ *His Excellency: George Washington.* 2004. Alfred A. Knopf. 320p. ISBN 1400040310.

George Washington (1732–1799) may not have been the smartest, best spoken, or most astute politician of his time, but according to Pulitzer Prize–winning author Joseph J. Ellis, he was the most ambitious. His vengeful resolve to beat the British, whom he blamed for his past business losses, carried the

Colonials to victory, and his determination that the young nation succeed kept the states together during his presidency. In this humanizing portrait of the revered Washington, Ellis explains why the Virginian was the central figure among a cast of talented men.

Frank, Katherine
Indira: The Life of Indira Nehru Gandhi. 2002. Houghton Mifflin. 567p. ISBN 039573097X.

Daughter of India's first prime minister after winning its independence from Great Britain, Indira Nehru Gandhi was groomed to be her country's leader. After attending prestigious schools, she studied the art of political compromise and became, for a time, a peacemaker between Hindus, Sikhs, and Muslims. After her first administration as prime minister failed, she reworked her alliances and returned to power. In this sympathetic political biography, Katherine Frank chronicles the career of a woman who believed herself India's greatest hope for peace and prosperity.

Goldstone, Nancy
The Lady Queen: The Notorious Reign of Joanna I, Queen of Naples, Jerusalem, and Sicily. 2009. Walker. 365p. ISBN 9780802716705.

Two centuries before Elizabeth I of England, Prince Andrew of Hungary and his wife Joanna I of Naples (1326–1382) succeeded her grandfather Robert the Wise to the throne of Naples. Andrew was soon murdered, and after being found innocent of his murder, 22-year-old Joanna assumed sole rule of diverse lands for more than 30 years. In this scholarly yet readable biography, historian Nancy Goldstone depicts Joanna as a passionate monarch, sure of her birthright, who outlived four husbands, supported the arts, built churches and hospitals, and expanded her realm before being assassinated.

Holmes, Richard
In the Footsteps of Churchill: A Study in Character. 2005. Basic Books. 351p. ISBN 0465030823.

By being bold and completely certain that he was absolutely right, Winston Churchill (1874–1965) won the confidence of the British people repeatedly throughout his long life. His quick and decisive actions also led to some horrendous blunders, such as the ill-fated Allied attack at Gallipoli in World War I. After each fall from power, he always rose again. In this frank assessment of his subject's successes and failures, military historian Richard Holmes examines the origins of Churchill's will to lead in perilous times.

Morris, Edmund
Theodore Rex. 2001. Random House. 772p. ISBN 0394555090. ಜ

Within weeks of assuming the office of president after the assassination of William McKinley, Theodore Roosevelt (1858–1919) introduced major antitrust legislation and an investigation into securities fraud. He also shocked his conservative supporters by inviting a black man to dinner at the White House. In his second book about Roosevelt, biographer Edmund Morris admiringly recounts seven-and-a-half busy years in the life of an energetic president.

Williams, Charles
The Last Great Frenchman: A Life of General de Gaulle. 1993. John Wiley & Sons. 544p. ISBN 0471117110.

Charles de Gaulle (1890–1970) is the dominant figure in 20th-century French history. His lone voice declaring "I am France" after the fall of his country to Germany in World War II rallied French resistance and restored French pride. He retired after the war, but later led his country away from a potentially disastrous civil war. In his admiring retelling of a hero's life, historian Charles Williams portrays de Gaulle as an autocratic and highly nationalistic leader who combined obstinacy and diplomacy to rebuild his war-torn country.

Wilson, Derek
Peter the Great. 2009. St. Martin's Press. 236p. ISBN 9780312550998.

After narrowly escaping execution by a mob at age 10 and enduring a power struggle among his siblings, Peter the Great (1672–1725) became de facto ruler of Russia at age 17 and was acknowledged as czar 7 years later. With a vision for modernizing his country, he initiated reforms in diplomacy, defense, government, education, and technology, and he spent lavishly on art and architecture. He even built a new capitol city to draw Russia nearer to Europe. In this lively historical biography, English novelist Derek Wilson tells how Peter not only remade Russia but also helped shape the modern world.

Politically Imperfect

To succeed in politics, an individual has to demonstrate the will and ability to negotiate with other people. Wheeling and dealing requires tolerance, flexibility, and determination. Success on the national stage also requires personal charisma. U.S. president John Quincy Adams, Chinese communist Zhou Enlai, and the other subjects in the following books tested their political skills in difficult times and for various reasons fell short of their goals.

Ackerman, Kenneth D.
Boss Tweed: The Rise and Fall of the Corrupt Pol Who Conceived the Soul of Modern New York. 2005. Carroll & Graf. 437p. ISBN 0786714352.

Mayor William Marcy "Boss" Tweed (1823–1878) was undeniably corrupt. He controlled not only New York City government but also governors, judges, and senators from several states, and lived an opulent life far beyond what the combined salaries from his various public offices would allow. Despite his avarice, he was beloved by the poor and working classes for whom he provided jobs and city services. Though Tweed was convicted and imprisoned for bribery and stealing public funds, former Washington bureaucrat Kenneth D. Ackerman portrays the fallen mayor as a prototype for many successful powerful politicians who followed.

Cooper, William J.
Jefferson Davis, American. 2000. Alfred A. Knopf. 757p. ISBN 0394569164.

The people of the Confederacy expected great leadership from their head of state, President Jefferson Davis (1808–1889). The champion of slavery and states' rights had been a hero in the war with Mexico, a powerful secretary of war under Franklin Pierce, and twice a senator from Mississippi. He could not, however, manage the Southern economy or supply the Confederate army under his command with food and ammunition. At war's end, he was captured and imprisoned. Southern historian William J. Cooper portrays Davis as a man who learned from failure and restored his influence but not his reputation in Reconstruction America.

Everitt, Anthony
Cicero: The Life and Times of Rome's Greatest Politician. 2001. Random House. 359p. ISBN 0375507469. 🐉

Upon the assassination of Julius Caesar, statesman Marcus Tillius Cicero (109–43 BCE) suspended the democratic rights of Roman citizens, losing the respect of his contemporaries and winning the admiration of future kings and presidents. Ironically, prior to this, the great orator had been the author and staunch defender of many of those same suspended rights. Using Cicero's speeches, essays, and letters, historian Anthony Everitt takes a close and sympathetic look at one of the most famous Roman citizens.

Gao Wenqian
Zhou Enlai: The Last Perfect Revolutionary, A Biography. 2007. Public Affair. 345p. ISBN: 9781586484156.

The reputation of Chinese revolutionary leader Zhou Enlai (1898–1976) has withstood tarnishing better than that of his contemporaries, including Mao Zedong. A new generation of Chinese writers, with the blessing of the new leaders, has exposed their predecessors' corruption and cruelty, but Zhou has retained the status of hero for saving many lives during the Cultural Revolution. In this behind-the-scenes biography recounting the long career of a survivor against the odds, expatriate Chinese biographer Gao Wenqian reveals that Zhou often grudgingly compromised his principles when Mao required his allegiance.

Heidler, David S., and Jeanne T. Heidler
Henry Clay: The Essential American. 2010. Random House. 595p. ISBN 9781400067268.

Along with John C. Calhoun and Daniel Webster, Kentucky statesman Henry Clay (1777–1852) was one of the three most important and long-serving members of the U.S. Senate during the first half of the 19th century. Known as a great debater and backroom dealer, Clay fostered laws on banking, transportation, westward expansion, defense, and slavery. Little could be accomplished without his approval, but he ultimately failed to become president and to find a compromise to hold his beloved country together. Admiring historians David S. Heidler and Jeanne T. Heidler recount the life of a man whose personal contradictions (a slave-owner who preached extending human rights) mirrored the country he served.

Isenberg, Nancy

Fallen Founder: The Life of Aaron Burr. 2007. Viking. 540p. ISBN 9780670063529.

New York statesman Aaron Burr (1756–1836) attained national prominence at an early age, becoming a senator at 35 and vice president at 45. He nearly became president in the flawed election of 1800, but his career suffered when he killed Alexander Hamilton in a duel. He fled to the Louisiana frontier where he may have plotted against the government, but eventually he returned to New York to become a rich lawyer. In this reassessing biography, Nancy Isenberg shows how history has been unkind to a man who was respected in his time.

Leamer, Laurence

Kennedy Men: 1901–1963: The Laws of the Father. 2001. William Morrow. 882p. ISBN: 9780688163150.

Having learned the ways of politics from his father, a Democratic ward boss for East Boston, Joseph Patrick Kennedy (1888–1969) groomed his four sons to be savvy statesmen who doggedly sought to gain influence first in Massachusetts and then in Washington. Critical mistakes, however, threatened to spoil their dreams. In the first of two epic biographies, journalist Laurence Leamer chronicles the public and private lives of five ambitious Kennedy men pursuing political power up to the assassination of President John F. Kennedy (1917–1963).

Wheelan, Joseph

▶ *Mr. Adams's Last Crusade: John Quincy Adams's Extraordinary Post-Presidential Life in Congress*. 2008. Public Affairs. 308p. ISBN 9780786720125.

As the sixth president of the United States, John Quincy Adams (1767–1848) could never rally his friends to beat his enemies. Like his father, Adams was too independent, often broke ranks with his party, and found allies hard to keep. His winning a congressional seat after losing the presidency was unexpected; little was expected of him in his final years. In this admiring biography, author Joseph Wheelan tells how Adams surprised his friends and critics, excelling as a dissenting voice raised against the expansion of slavery into the nation's territories.

Charismatic Spirits

All influential people, whether in business, the arts, the military, or politics, are in the business of persuasion. In person or through print or electronic media, they try to convince their readers, listeners, or viewers of their concern, vision, and trustworthiness. An infectious smile helps, as do well-chosen and sincerely delivered words. Still, rare are the individuals, such as U.S. president Ronald Reagan or travel writer Bruce Chatwin, who can charm the public and gain the trust of strangers. The following books identify charismatic individuals who have used their gifts for good, evil, or both.

Eliot, Marc
▶ *Reagan: The Hollywood Years*. 2008. Harmony Books. 375p. ISBN 9780307405128.

The films of Ronald Reagan (1911–2004) are widely acclaimed as forgettable and most are rarely shown today. Though in 30 years as an actor Reagan won little praise and landed few starring roles of note, he left Hollywood having charmed and impressed American moviegoers and television viewers as a level-headed neighbor worthy of their trust. In this quick read, celebrity biographer Marc Eliot tells how through his movie roles and work for the Screen Actors Guild Reagan shaped a winning political persona.

Goldsworthy, Adrian Keith
Caesar: Life of a Colossus. 2006. Yale University Press. 583p. ISBN 9780300120486.

Julius Caesar (100–44 BC) lived in one of Rome's most chaotic times. As a youth, he survived being tried for treason and being kidnapped by pirates to become a highly decorated military leader. As a passionate orator, he controlled the Senate and seduced many of his opponents' wives. His assassination stunned his followers who immediately deified him. In this epic biography, historian Adrian Goldsworthy depicts Julius Caesar as a talented and ambitious leader who recovered from missteps to become the Roman Empire's most powerful man.

Heller, Anne C.
Ayn Rand and the World She Made. 2009. Nan A. Talese. 567p. ISBN 9780385513999.

After escaping from the Soviet Union at 21, screenwriter and novelist Ayn Rand (1905–1982) became a champion for capitalism in her adopted American homeland. Through her novels *Atlas Shrugged* and *The Fountainhead* and popular essays, she drew like-minded people into the fight she led against socialists bent on limiting personal wealth. Intensely jealous, Rand demanded devotion from friends and lovers. In this mostly sympathetic biography, business journalist Anne C. Heller recounts the turbulent personal life of a charismatic thinker who influenced presidents and others, such as Federal Reserve Chairman Alan Greenspan.

Jackson, Blair
Garcia: An American Life. 1999. Viking. 498p. ISBN 0670886602.

Music journalist Blair Jackson admits that he is not dispassionate about his subject in this biography of rock musician Jerry Garcia (1942–1995) of the Grateful Dead. Jackson calls himself a Deadhead. Though he writes candidly about the free-spirited and experimental lifestyle of Garcia in drug-permeated San Francisco, the author's focus is Garcia's musical vision and charisma, fondly recalling how through countless recording sessions and concert tours Garcia became the Pied Piper of psychedelic culture.

Randal, Jonathan
Osama: The Making of a Terrorist. 2004. Knopf. 339p. ISBN 0375409017. ☙

Author Jonathan Randal had been attempting to interview Osama bin Laden (1957–2011) for several years when American authorities reported that the shadowy financier of Arab terrorism had directed the bombing of the USS *Cole*. Randal had gotten close to his goal several times and had even received a humorous note supposedly from bin Laden himself. Knowing then that he would never meet the Saudi terrorist, he continued collecting stories from associates and enemies. The result is this fascinating account of a man who with little more than an obsession and devoted followers has polarized the world.

Shakespeare, Nicholas
Bruce Chatwin. 1999. Doubleday. 618p. ISBN 0385498292.

World traveler Bruce Chatwin (1940–1989), author of *On Patagonia* and *The Viceroy of Ouidah*, could charm almost anyone, even when he could not speak their language. The self-assured Chatwin would arrive in the remotest stations of Asia, Africa, or South America and quickly win the confidence of local tribesmen and their chiefs, as well as anthropologists, archeologists, and paleontologists eager to tell their stories. Though stricken with AIDS, he kept a hectic schedule of travel and writing until his death. With admiration, novelist Nicholas Shakespeare recounts the career of a magnetic character who loved the world's least-known places.

Unger, Miles J.
Magnifico: The Brilliant Life and Violent Times of Lorenzo de' Medici. 2008. Simon & Schuster. 513p. ISBN 97807443254342.

As heir to his family's wealth, Lorenzo de' Medici (1449–1492) served as unofficial ruler of Florence at the height of the Renaissance, the time of great art from artists such as Leonardo, Botticelli, and Michelangelo. As a generous patron to painters, sculptors, and architects, Lorenzo oversaw a glorious transformation of his city. Within that city's walls, however, as well as in neighboring Italian states, there were many enemies and assassins to keep at bay. Art historian Miles J. Unger recounts how the astute Lorenzo combined political charm, financial power, and ruthless acts to stay the most powerful figure of his day.

Weller, Sam
The Bradbury Chronicles: The Life of Ray Bradbury. 2005. William Morrow. 384p. ISBN 006054581X.
   Born in the American Midwest, absorbing popular culture from the moment of his birth (which he claimed to remember), popular fiction writer Ray Bradbury (1920–) became an international guru for imagination. Not an optimist but a believer in optimal behavior, Bradbury saw in the world around him evil to expose and good to champion. Through pulp fiction, horror, science fiction, fantasy, radio plays, comic books, and movies, he reached every generation since World War II. Journalist and devoted fan Sam Weller intimately recounts Bradbury's creative life and its cultural impact.

Genius Personified

A genius not only sees what others overlook and understands what others do not, he or she reveals the unknown to all. Often a display of brilliance, whether it is an Albert Einstein theory or an Irving Berlin show tune, is resented by those whose work is outshone. The men and women who accept the role of genius have to be determined and thick-skinned to succeed. Here are stories of people with the ambition to become masters of the arts, business, literature, and science.

Ackroyd, Peter
J.M.W. Turner. 2006. Doubleday. 173p. ISBN 0385507984.
   Painter Joseph Mallord William Turner (1775–1851) brushed off admirers' praises with the claim that his genius was nothing but hard work, but he was not humble. He still expected the best space for hanging his pictures at annual Royal Academy exhibitions. Often alone, never married, England's master of marine, landscape, and historical painting was not totally unsociable; he cared for his father and attached himself to widows. In this admiring compact biography, author Peter Ackroyd chronicles Turner's revolutionary career as the painter obsessed with light and color.

Aczel, Amir D.
Pendulum: Léon Foucault and the Triumph of Science. 2003. Atria Books. 275p. ISBN 0743464788.
   Praise for his accomplishments came late for self-taught physicist Léon Foucault (1819–1868). The elite of the French scientific community tried to ignore the inventor of new telescopes, photographic processing techniques, and the gyroscope; he was not of their class and training. They were stunned when he dramatically used a large pendulum to prove that the earth rotates on

an axis, something both Galileo and Newton had failed to do. In this quick-reading biography, science writer Amir D. Aczel recounts the brief hard-fought life of a naturally brilliant thinker.

Beyer, Kurt W.
Grace Hopper and the Invention of the Information Age. 2009. MIT Press. 388p. ISBN 9780262013109. ☙

In the aftermath of World War I, Grace Hopper (1906–1992) joined other upper class women pursuing academic careers and became a respected mathematics professor at Vassar College. When Japanese bombers attacked Pearl Harbor in 1941, she joined the U.S. Navy and was assigned to the Computation Laboratory at Harvard University to work with Mark I and Mark II computers. Known now as the Mother of COBOL, she soon recognized that programming was as important as the physical structure of computers. In this detailed science biography, author Kurt W. Beyer tells how through a mixture of accommodation and rebellion Hopper overcame gender bias, advanced programming languages, and won an appointment as an admiral in the U.S. Navy.

Brian, Denis
Pulitzer: A Life. 2001. John Wiley & Sons. 438p. ISBN 0471332003.

Between the time of the U.S. Civil War and the start of World War I, newspaper publisher Joseph Pulitzer (1847–1911) defined the news. Not only was he sending reporters around the world to gather stories, he was also directing investigators to uncover corruption in business and politics. Ambitious to sell newspapers and influence public policy, he made enemies of many important public figures, including President Theodore Roosevelt and publishing competitor William Randolph Hearst. Drawing from the publisher's letters and interviews, biographer Denis Brian portrays Pulitzer as a moral man and the mastermind of modern journalism.

Isaacson, Walter
▶ *Einstein: His Life and Universe*. 2007. Simon & Schuster. 675p. ISBN 9780743264730. ☹

Albert Einstein (1879–1955) was only a lowly paid patent clerk in 1905 when he published five brilliant articles that challenged Newtonian physics and became the basis of the science of quantum physics and the concept of relativity. Though fame came to him quickly, he spent many years struggling with prejudice against Jews to attain academic appointments, and he failed to discover the unified theory that he believed would reconcile nuclear, electromagnetic, and gravitational forces. Readers do not have to understand science to enjoy this epic biography of an unlikely celebrity.

Jablonski, Edward
Irving Berlin: American Troubadour. 1999. Henry Holt and Company. 406p. ISBN 080504077.

Although he never learned to read music, Irving Berlin (1888–1989) wrote more than 1,500 songs and is celebrated as a master of the Broadway musical.

Born into poverty in Russia, he started his music career as a singing waiter in Chinatown in New York City, writing ditties and getting noticed by the newspaper reporters. With this break, he began writing hit songs, such as "Cheek to Cheek" and "White Christmas," and socializing with musical elites, such as the Gershwins, Cole Porter, Fred Astaire, and Ethel Mermen. Admiring author Edward Jablonski tells how life was mostly good for Berlin until old age and the rock 'n' roll era, which the songwriter despised.

Kunhardt, Philip B., Jr., Philip B. Kunhardt III, and Peter W. Kunhardt
  P. T. Barnum: America's Greatest Showman. 1995. Alfred A. Knopf. 358p. ISBN 0679435743.
    P. T. Barnum (1810–1891) is often depicted as a hefty man with a cigar—the familiar image of 19th-century success. Unlike the millionaire industrialists that he resembled, however, he made his fortune in show business. With his circuses, museums, and theaters, Barnum seemed to anticipate each new wave of popular entertainment. In this heavily illustrated biography, the authors not only recount Barnum's genius for promotion but also defend their subject against contemporary criticisms of hucksterism and exploitation.

Stross, Randall
  The Wizard of Menlo Park: How Thomas Alva Edison Invented the Modern World. 2007. Crown. 376p. ISBN 9781400047628.
    Could anyone who designed concrete furniture be called a genius? Inventor and industrialist Thomas Alva Edison (1847–1931), who often rejected advice from his board and employees, almost lost his company promoting this molded furniture. Yet, the owner of more than 1,000 patents is still regarded highly for inventing the microphone, phonograph, incandescent light bulb, and many other modern devices. In this candid narrative, author Randall Stross examines a man whose stubbornness and pride nearly derailed his business.

Changelings

Individuals unhappy with their lives sometimes change them radically by starting new careers or moving to new places. Trying to erase their former selves, they may even adopt new names, such as author P. L. Travers or pilot Jackie Cochran. If their new personas fail to satisfy, they may try another. The following biographies feature famous people of ever-changing character.

Bolt, Rodney
  The Librettist of Venice: The Remarkable Life of Lorenzo da Ponte. 2006. Bloomsbury. 428p. ISBN 9781596911185.
    How did a poor boy from the Jewish ghetto of 18th-century Venice become a wayward Catholic priest and companion to Giacomo Casanova, the famous seducer of high society women? How did he then, after a spell as the librettist for Wolfgang Amadeus Mozart, remake himself as a professor of Italian studies at

Columbia College in New York, while doubling as an opera impresario? With much gentle humor, author Rodney Bolt recounts the story of Lorenzo da Ponte (1749–1838), a cleverly deceptive man who could be whoever he wanted to be.

Kahn, Roger

A Flame of Pure Fire: Jack Dempsey and the Roaring '20s. 1999. Harcourt Brace. 473p. ISBN 0151002967. ☙

For boxer Jack Dempsey (1895–1983), life was a series of transitions, all aimed at success. As a miner, a cowboy, and even a hobo, the determined young man was training himself for prize fights that he could only imagine. After many years and many defeats, he finally prevailed and became heavyweight boxing champion of the world. In this admiring biography focused on the pivotal decade of the boxer's life, veteran sports journalist Roger Kahn tells how Dempsey then used his hard-won boxing fame to become an actor and a prosperous businessman.

Lawson, Valerie

Mary Poppins, She Wrote: The Life of P.L. Travers. 2006. Simon & Schuster. 401p. ISBN 9780743298162.

In the quest for magic and mystical experience, Australian Helen Lyndon Goff (1899–1996), known as P.L. Travers, transformed herself from an unhappy child into a dancer, then an actress, and finally a writer of children's stories, including the long-running Mary Poppins series. She also moved through her self-defined stages of a woman's life—nymph, mother, and crone—while seeking gurus to replace the father who had never met her expectations. In this psychological biography, New Zealand journalist Valerie Lawson examines the life and writings of a woman who said she wanted no biography, but then left all her highly organized papers for scholars to read.

Nicholl, Charles

Somebody Else: Arthur Rimbaud in Africa, 1880–1891. 1999. University of Chicago Press. 333p. ISBN 0226580296.

After losing interest in writing poetry, bohemian French poet Arthur Rimbaud (1854–1891) traveled to the Middle East to sample Arab culture. In the next 11 years, he often assumed local dress to wander through Yemen, Ethiopia, and Egypt as a trader. Besides dealing in coffee, spices, and cloth, he tried his hand as a soldier of fortune, gunrunner, and slave trader. In this literary biography, author Charles Nicholl recounts the known and rumored events of a short and secretive life.

Phillips, Julie

▶ *James Tiptree, Jr.: The Double Life of Alice B. Sheldon*. 2006. St. Martin's Press. 469p. ISBN 9780312203856. ȣ

In her 60s, Alice B. Sheldon (1915–1987) was thought to be just a woman living in a quiet suburb outside Washington, D.C. Few people knew that she has been an artist, WAC officer, CIA agent, chicken farmer, and research psychologist. This daughter of the romance novelist Mary Bradley had another secret—she was the mysterious science fiction novelist known as James Tiptree Jr. In this psychiatric biography, author Julie Phillips examines a complicated woman who reinvented herself regularly.

Rich, Doris L.
Jackie Cochran: Pilot in the Fast Lane. 2007. University of Florida Press. 279p. ISBN 9780813030432.

Known as Bessie Smith in impoverished rural Florida, Jackie Cochran (1906–1980) transformed herself, through hard work and astute marketing, into a highly successful and rich cosmetics executive at the height of the Great Depression. Then, she quit her Manhattan office to become a pilot competing with Amelia Earhart for aviation records. With candor and admiration, author Doris L. Rich recounts the divergent life of a tenacious woman who eventually became friends with Presidents Eisenhower and Johnson.

Stape, John
The Several Lives of Joseph Conrad. 2007. Pantheon Books. 369p. ISBN 9781400044498.

Known later as novelist Joseph Conrad (1857–1924), Józef Teodor Konrad Korzeniowski was born Polish when there was no Poland. His childhood was spent in war-torn cities of the Ukraine and Eastern Europe that are difficult for modern readers to identify. As a desperate adolescent, he went to sea, eventually reaching remote and dangerous places, such as China, Indonesia, and Africa. Using newly available letters that correct many misconceptions, Conrad scholar John Stape intimately tells how after all these experiences, Conrad became an English citizen with a typical family and author of popular adventure stories.

Williams, Kate
England's Mistress: The Infamous Life of Emma Hamilton. 2006. Ballantine Books. 415p. ISBN 0345461940.

Lady Emma Hamilton (1765–1815) led an incredible life. As the daughter of a blacksmith in a coal-mining town in western England, Amy Lyon was destined for a hard life as a serving woman. At age 12, she was an unsalaried maid, working for meals and a bed, but she was soon dismissed and went to London to seek work. Ever an opportunist, she became a highly visible model, actress, and courtesan who then moved to exotic Naples where she transformed herself into a lady of society and married an aged ambassador. With admiration, cultural historian Kate Williams portrays Hamilton as a heroine worthy of the attention she gained as mistress to Admiral Horatio Nelson.

Eccentric Egos

Most people try to fit in. They blend into their society, adopting the habits of the people around them, never drawing any attention to themselves. Few of these people are ever the subjects of biographies. Others, such as cartoonist

Charles Addams, rock musician Frank Zappa, or architect Antoni Gaudi, act oddly, pursuing their own goals and portraying themselves as different from common folk. In the process, they may excel in their professions and lead singular lives worthy of biographies.

Davis, Linda H.
Chas Addams: A Cartoonist's Life. 2006. Random House. 382p. ISBN 0679463259.

New Yorker cartoonist Charles Addams (1912–1988) encouraged wild rumors about his private life by wearing antique clothes, driving fabulous cars, and lacing his conversation with gloomy and gruesome thoughts. A mastermind of the morbid, he was even said to sleep in a coffin. In this entertaining biography, Linda H. Davis reveals that the extroverted Addams had an insatiable love of women and wine as well as werewolves and witches.

Gibson, Ian
The Shameful Life of Salvador Dalí. 1997. W. W. Norton & Company. 798p. ISBN 0393046249.

Artist Salvador Dalí was a self-proclaimed genius. Through his bizarre art, strange behaviors, and mythologizing autobiographical writings, he captured public attention and promoted himself as an intellectual jester. His persona, however, was just an act to hide his insecurity and tendency to blush. Mixing psychological biography and art criticism, author Ian Gibson describes how a successful exploiter of popular culture became a victim of his own con game.

Hawkes, David
John Milton: A Hero of Our Time. 2010. Counterpoint. 354p. ISBN 9781582434377.

English poet John Milton (1608–1674) believed that he was a prophet with a strong message of hope for future readers. According to literary scholar David Hawkes, Milton was less interested in his contemporaries, whom he judged to be filled with avarice and conceit, than in coming generations, which he hoped would be free-thinking and spiritual. With such an isolating attitude, he found living in 17th-century England difficult. In this philosophical biography, Hawkes examines the public and private Milton, revealing him to be a very modern thinker who might have flourished in a later time.

Miles, Barry
Zappa: A Biography. 2004. Grove Press. 464p. ISBN 080211783X.

After being entrapped by an undercover policeman for making a sexually suggestive audio recording, struggling musician Frank Zappa (1940–1993) rejected "the American way of life," according to rock music biographer Barry Miles. From that moment in 1965, Zappa insisted on full control of his music and his life, freeing himself to lampoon authority and ridicule what he saw as hypocrisy. In this sympathetic biography, Miles chronicles the strange life of a rock musician who loved his wife and children, desperately wanted to compose classical music, and became an unlikely official U.S. representative of the Czechoslovakian government. Some readers may find scenes and language offensive.

Shelden, Michael

▶ *Mark Twain: Man in White: The Grand Adventure of His Final Years*. Random House, 2010. 484p. ISBN 9780679448006. ⧽

In 1906, when fashionable men dressed in black or gray, Mark Twain (1835–1910) switched to all white regardless of season. He stood before Congress, attended operas, strolled along the streets of New York, and helped open the World's Fair in Virginia while wearing an inappropriate white suit. Only this beloved and aging author could thumb his nose at convention so easily. Some biographers have described Mark Twain in his final years, when one of his daughters died and he fired his dishonest housekeeper and accountant, as depressed and helpless. In this frank but admiring biography, Michael Shelden disagrees, portraying the author as a funny man defeating tragedy by living for honesty and pleasure.

Van Hensbergen, Gijs

Gaudi. 2001. HarperCollins, 322p. ISBN 0066210658.

When Catalonians saw eccentric architect Antoni Gaudi (1852–1926) walking on a street in Barcelona, they often crossed to the other side to avoid conversation. He might beg donations to continue his extravagant projects, praised by modernist Le Corbusier, but ridiculed by traditionalist architects. Still, Catalonians revered him as a hero at a time when the Spanish government outlawed the regional language. In his sympathetic and well-illustrated biography of Gaudi, author Gijs Van Hensbergen portrays the designer of organic architecture as an impractical man whose works are still controversial.

Wilkinson, Alec

The Happiest Man in the World: An Account of the Life of Poppa Neutrino. 2007. Random House. 301p. ISBN 9781400065431.

In the early 1980s, a dog bite nearly killed wanderer David Pearlman (1933–2011). After two years of life-threatening illnesses, the remarkable musician, polymath, and former preacher recovered and celebrated by changing his name to Poppa Neutrino. He then built a raft from garbage, which he sailed across the Atlantic Ocean. In this conversation-filled account, rock musician and *New Yorker* contributor Alec Wilkinson describes the life and work of a world traveler who believed in the pursuit of happiness.

Winchester, Simon

The Man Who Loved China: The Fantastic Story of the Eccentric Scientist Who Unlocked the Mysteries of Middle Kingdom. 2008. HarperCollins. 316p. ISBN 9780060884598. ⧽

Throughout his career, biochemist Joseph Needham (1900–1995) alienated conservative colleagues by espousing nonconformist scientific and political ideas. He was an early supporter of Communist causes and a proponent of open marriage, never hiding his affair with a Chinese scientist. He traveled extensively in China during the dangerous Japanese occupation of World War II, seeking evidence to prove that the poor backward country had once been rich with scientific knowledge and invention. Popular science author Simon Winchester depicts Needham as uncommonly devoted to his unpopular academic pursuits in this entertaining biography.

Fatally Flawed

Some people seem bent upon self-destructive behaviors that are obviously going to lead to tragedy. Friends and family try to intervene, but the reckless remain without regard for their own safety and well being. Making sense of their flawed lives seems next to impossible, but human curiosity is boundless. Readers continue to want to know about tragic figures, such as macabre author Edgar Allan Poe and hard-living country singer Johnny Cash. Here are some compelling biographies of out-of-control characters.

Ackroyd, Peter
▶ *Poe: A Life Cut Short*. 2008. Nan A. Talese/Doubleday. 205p. ISBN 9780385508001.

Poet and short story writer Edgar Allan Poe (1809–1849) could be a poster child for the fatally flawed. He gambled, took drugs, drank excessively, married his 13-year-old cousin, and was obsessed about being recognized as a great writer. Just when he pulled himself together, he fell apart again. Literary novelist, critic, and historian Peter Ackroyd distills the essential Poe into this quick reading story that most biography readers will enjoy.

Bailey, Blake
Cheever: A Life. **2009**. **Alfred A. Knopf. 770p. ISBN 9781400043941**. ⅃

Despite acclaim for his short stories and novels and being accepted in an elite circle of literary figures, John Cheever (1912–1982) suffered great self-doubt. "I came from nowhere and I don't know where I'm going." Ironically, he was from a deep-rooted New England family that he wished to escape. Ashamed of how he neglected and betrayed his wife and children, he drank excessively. Cheever scholar Blake Bailey draws heavily from diaries and letters in this detailed year-by-year account of a guilt-ridden man.

Benjaminson, Peter
The Lost Supreme: The Life of Dreamgirl Florence Ballard. 2008. 213p. ISBN 9781556527050.

After reading his short account in the Detroit Free Press about how she and her children were living on welfare, former member of the Supremes Flo Ballard (1943–1976) invited reporter Peter Benjaminson to hear her full story. More than 30 years later, long after the singer's tragic heart attack at 32, Benjaminson incorporated that interview into this sympathetic biography of a young woman whose musical career was derailed by alcohol, drugs, bad management, and conflicts with Supremes lead singer Diana Ross and Motown Records.

Fuller, Alexandra

The Legend of Colton H. Bryant. 2008. Penguin Press. 202p. ISBN 9781594201837. ☙

Wyoming roughneck Colton H. Bryant (1980–2006) knew only one speed—fast. As a boy, he often landed in the hospital emergency room, and as a young man, he totaled cars. His early death seemed predestined. In this intimate biography of an ill-fated employee for an industry with a locally poor safety record, author Alexandra Fuller portrays Bryant as a working-class character who would do anything for his friends and family—except slow down.

Meyers, Jeffrey

Inherited Risk: Errol and Sean Flynn in Hollywood and Vietnam. 2002. Simon & Schuster. 368p. ISBN 0743210905.

Nurture or nature? Actor Errol Flynn (1909–1959) was a romantic leading man who took the persona of his swashbuckling roles to heart, leading a promiscuous, alcoholic life, dying prematurely at 50. His son Sean Flynn (1941–1970?) was a wild pot-smoking youth who appeared in eight movies, went to Vietnam as a war photographer, disappeared, and was presumed dead at 29. Through sad stories of reckless behavior, biographer Jeffrey Meyers depicts the tragic parallel lives of a father and a son.

Osborne, Frances

The Bolter. 2009. Alfred A. Knopf. 300p. ISBN 9780307270146.

Idina Sackville (1893–1955) appeared to be the obedient daughter of an aristocratic family when she married a young and wealthy cavalry officer just before the outbreak of World War I. Her seemingly assured happy life was quickly lost. Her loveless husband's infidelity drove her out of their never-completed villa and into a series of scandalous affairs and brief marriages in Kenya's Happy Valley. Sackville's great granddaughter Frances Osborne quotes family letters in recounting the directionless and drunken life of an Edwardian belle in Britain's African colonies.

Seward, Desmond

Caravaggio: A Passionate Life. 1999. William Morrow. 202p. ISBN 0688150322.

Despite the favor that his exquisite paintings won from cardinals and the pope, Italian artist Michelangelo Merisi da Caravaggio (1573–1610) lived in fear of assassination. Being a man with an uncontrollable temper, he made enemies easily and had even killed a man in a duel. Did he truly die from exhaustion or was he secretly murdered? In this investigative biography, historian Desmond Seward examines Caravaggio's artistic achievement and violent events that shortened the brilliant painter's life.

Streissguth, Michael
Johnny Cash: The Biography. 2006. **Da Capo Press, 334p. ISBN: 9780306813689.**
Singer Johnny Cash (1932–2003) was complicated and unruly. His pursuit of fame tore his first marriage apart, and being either stoned or drunk he ruined and canceled many performances. He even went to prison for smuggling drugs. Despite the severity of his faults, he was often forgiven and is still loved by country music fans worldwide. In this candid yet sympathetic biography, Michael Streissguth recounts the life of one of country music's biggest and most troubled stars.

Rebels with Causes

Much is wrong with the world, and some impassioned people feel compelled to challenge the status quo to set the world right. They stand up against ridicule and isolation to push their causes, which may or may not be appreciated by the general populace. Some may even risk their lives and liberty to bring down governments that they view as oppressive. The following biographies examine the lives and motives of author Oscar Wilde, comedian Lenny Bruce, revolutionary Guiseppe Garibaldi, and other rebelling individuals.

Balf, Todd
Major: A Black Athlete, a White Era, and the Fight to Be the World's Fastest Human Being. 2008. Crown. 306p. ISBN 9780307236586.
African American bicyclist Marshall Taylor (1878–1932) began his career in the brief moment before professional sports began banning blacks. His string of major victories over white racers may have even contributed to the call for racial prohibitions. After his exclusion, Taylor joined races by secretly lining up behind starting lines; he would catch up and defiantly pass the official contestants. Journalist Todd Balf recounts the life of an audacious rebel forgotten by most sports and civil rights historians.

Belford, Barbara
▶ *Oscar Wilde: A Certain Genius*. 2000. Random House. 381p. ISBN 0679457348.
The life of playwright Oscar Wilde (1854–1900) is often written as an entertaining tragedy. His quips make readers laugh, and his arrest, imprisonment, and disgrace for being exposed as a homosexual make them cry. In most of these accounts, Wilde died a broken man. In her examination of Wilde and his writings, author Barbara Belford tells a different story—that of a man who bravely lived as he pleased, supporting a cause too radical for his time.

Collins, Robert K. L., and David M. Skover
The Trials of Lenny Bruce: The Fall and Rise of an American Icon. 2002. Sourcebooks, Inc. 562p. ISBN 1570719861.

Does the right to free speech extend to obscenity? Comedian Lenny Bruce (1925–1966) believed that it did and risked his career by relentlessly incorporating offensive material in his routines to test the law. By doing so, he lost most of his friends and subjected himself to constant criticism. In this candid account of Bruce's desperate campaign, legal historians Robert K. L. Collins and David M. Skover recount the decline, death, and posthumous fame of a modern rebel.

Lawday, David
The Giant of the French Revolution: Danton, a Life. 2009. Grove Press. 294p. ISBN 9780802119339.

In storming the Bastille, Georges-Jacques Danton (1759–1794) and a host of rebels brought an end to a thousand years of French monarchy. Creating a new government, however, proved more difficult. Taller than most and able to speak eloquently for hours about the cause, Danton was a leader who initially supported violent action to fuel the revolution, but who eventually pleaded for moderation and mercy. In this frank biography, journalist David Lawday portrays the larger-than-life rebel as a key player and tragic victim of his time.

Reynolds, David S.
John Brown, Abolitionist: The Man Who Killed Slavery, Sparked the Civil War, and Seeded Civil Rights. 2005. Knopf. 578p. ISBN 0375411887. ♻ ☃

Believing that the end justifies violent means, abolitionist John Brown (1800–1859) served as a self-appointed avenging angel rallying moral people to end slavery in the United States. His raid on the federal arsenal at Harpers Ferry, Virginia, divided abolitionists, shocked Southern slaveholders, and set the stage for the larger armed conflict that tore the nation. In this sympathetic biography, author David S. Reynolds describes a man unshakably committed to a heartfelt cause for which he was willing to die.

Scirocco, Alfonso
Garibaldi: Citizen of the World: A Biography. 2007. Princeton University Press. 442p. ISBN 9780691115405.

Born in France in 1807, Guiseppe Garibaldi was the world's most famous revolutionary of the 19th century. After a failed uprising in Genoa, Italy, in 1834, he was exiled to South America where he fought for the Republic of Rio Grande do Sul against Brazil and for Uruguay against Argentina. He returned to Europe to fight for a number of losing causes before helping unify Italy. In this admiring biography, Alfonso Scirocco describes Garibaldi as an idealist without ideology who survived many wars to write novels and to lecture in support of further revolution.

Service, Robert
Trotsky: A Biography. 2009. Belknap Press. 600p. ISBN 9780674036154.

    The alliance of Russian revolutionary Leon Trotsky (1879–1940) with Vladimir Lenin's Bolsheviks was always tenuous. In the struggle for power after Lenin's death, Trotsky lost to Joseph Stalin and was expelled from the Soviet Union. In light of Stalin's brutality and the assassination of Trotsky in Mexico, a myth of the rebel as the good communist who would have led his country to a more just society grew among his admirers worldwide. Using newly released Soviet documents, historian Robert Service lucidly debates whether Trotsky deserves his martyr's reputation.

Zinovieff, Sofka
Red Princess: A Revolutionary Life. 2008. Pegasus Books. 346p. ISBN 9781605980096.

    Descended from Catherine the Great, Sofka Dolgorouky (1907–1994) was born into Russian aristocracy, but she was in exile by 10. Ironically, after living a life of privilege in London and Paris and fighting for the French Underground during World War II, she turned to communism. Drawing from Dolgorouky's old Russian diary and her own discoveries, granddaughter Sofka Zinovieff reports on a dramatic life full of love and revolution.

Outrageous Rule Breakers

    "Rules? Of course, they are needed. But they don't apply to me." That statement sums up the attitude of the individuals whose lives are recounted in the following books. They felt special and free to do what they pleased without regard for others. Their flaunting of laws and societal rules were widely reported in their time, and many of them are still remembered for their outrageous behavior. While entertaining, these biographies of stuntman Evel Knievel, LSD guru Timothy Leary, and other rule breakers could also be called cautionary tales.

Barker, Stuart
Evel Knievel: Life of Evel. 2008. St. Martin's Press. 323p. ISBN 9780312547356.

    The laws of physics were not the only rules that stuntman Evel Knievel (1938–2007) dared to break. The entertainer from the bad side of Butte, Montana, broke his vows of marriage repeatedly, tried to live on bourbon, and was arrested at various times for robbery, assault and battery, and income tax evasion. Incredibly, his bravado in the wake of arrests only made him more famous and led to friendships with Elvis Presley and Frank Sinatra. In this frank biography, sports writer Stuart Barker portrays Knievel as an often-injured free spirit obsessed with self-promotion.

Fraser, Flora
Pauline Bonaparte: Venus of Empire. 2009. Alfred A. Knopf. 287p. ISBN: 9780307265449.

Pauline Bonaparte (1780–1825) was said to be the best dressed and most beautiful woman in Europe. As such, she was sought as a model by painters and sculptors, and because of her notorious behavior, she was often the subject of gossip—much of it true. As sister of Napoleon Bonaparte, the emperor of France, she lived a life of luxury until he fell from power. Historical biographer Flora Fraser, who has written about many strong and unruly women, recounts the life of a woman who rejected social mores but was loyal to her brother, even in exile.

French, Patrick
The World Is What It Is: The Authorized Biography of V. S. Naipaul. 2008. Alfred A. Knopf. 554p. ISBN 9781400044054.

If you are a friend of V. S. Naipaul (1932–), you must have thick skin. The author from an Indian family born in Trinidad is easily insulted and ready to retaliate. While his novels and nonfiction show critical understanding of world cultures and the plight of individuals, statements he makes in public are often perceived as crass and bigoted. Having unlimited access to Naipaul's papers, authorized biographer Patrick French presents a frank yet sympathetic portrait of a complicated man who has broken with his heritage and rarely tries to conform to his chosen society.

Greenfield, Robert
Timothy Leary: A Biography. 2006. Harcourt. 689p. ISBN 9780151005000.

Celebrated proponent of LSD, Timothy Leary (1920–1996) began skirting rules and defying authority at an early age. Through clever deceit, he was able to pass through military training in World War II without learning to fire a weapon. As a professor at the University of California at Berkeley and Harvard University, he began experiments on the recreational use of drugs and became companion to beats and hippies. In this detailed exposé, author Robert Greenfield recounts how a wayward academic became the guru of a cultural revolution.

Levine, Robert
Maria Callas: A Musical Biography. 2003. Black Dog & Leventhal Publishers. 224p. ISBN 1579122833.

On stage and off, glamorous soprano Maria Callas made headlines. She drew crowds to hear her sing opera's most romantic and tragic roles, thrilling listeners with performances that some colleagues warned would ruin her voice. Offstage, she fought with directors, attended swank parties, shopped in exclusive shops, and flirted with wealthy married men. In this heavily illustrated biography that includes two compact discs of Callas's performances, author Robert Levine chronicles her always-tumultuous life and praises her artistry.

O'Brien, Edna

▶ *Byron in Love: A Short Daring Life*. 2009. W. W. Norton. 227p. ISBN 9780393070118.

Women swooned at the sight of Lord George Gordon Byron, the poet known as Lord Byron (1788–1824). Like the legendary Don Juan, the British peer traveled across Europe, keeping lists of the women he seduced; he turned these exploits into poems published for all of English society to read. Novelist Edna O'Brien recounts the many affairs of a self-centered but obviously charming man who died an inglorious death for the romantic cause of Greek liberation.

Pearson, Roger

Voltaire Almighty: A Life in Pursuit of Freedom. 2005. Bloomsbury. 447p. ISBN 1582346305. ⋑

French author and philosopher Voltaire (1694–1778) relished conflict with political and religious authorities. Throughout his long life, he challenged censors, monarchs, and critics by willfully seducing married women, smuggling books, gambling, and writing controversial plays and verse. To Voltaire, imprisonment and exile from France were just the price he had to pay for pursuing personal freedom. In this stylish biography, which borrows chapter headings from Voltaire's own work, author Roger Pearson offers Voltaire as a model for future libertines.

Seymour, Miranda

Bugatti Queen: In Search of a French Racing Legend. 2004. Random House. 323p. ISBN 1400061687.

A rural postmaster's daughter who left her village for the glitter of Paris, Hellé Nice (1900–1984) tried dancing and modeling before convincing Italian car manufacturer Ettore Bugatti to let her drive his racing cars. Wishing to be the fastest woman in the world, she took risks that led to an accident that ended her career. Describing Nice as a reckless woman with many lovers and who collaborated with the Nazis in World War II, Miranda Seymour recounts a frenetic life that ended in poverty and shame.

Evil Incarnate

Is anyone truly evil? Were Soviet leader Joseph Stalin or the Reverend Jim Jones thoroughly malevolent? The authors of the following biographies would probably answer "yes." The biographers tell the stories of seemingly heartless individuals who relished the harm that they did to others, whether it be physical or psychological. Criminals and dictators dominate the group, but there are others who lured their victims with promises of friendship or heavenly bliss. Readers may shudder.

Carlo, Philip
The Butcher: Anatomy of a Mafia Psychopath. 2009. William Morrow. 298p.
ISBN 9780061744655.

Mafia assassin and Brooklyn drug kingpin Tommy Pitera (1954–) is reported to have killed 60 people. Associates portrayed the hit man for hire as
both businesslike and brutal, a killer with no regrets. Even though he is in
prison now serving a life sentence, he has shown no remorse and named no clients. Having grown up in the same neighborhood as his subject, noted criminal
biographer Philip Carlo graphically describes the making and downfall of one
of organized crime's most dangerous men.

Dudgeon, Piers
Neverland: J. M. Barrie, the du Mauriers, and the Dark Side of Peter Pan.
2009. Pegasus Books. 333p. ISBN 9781605980638. ⧩

After discovering that novelist Daphne du Maurier had sealed her adolescent diaries for 50 years after her death, curious author Piers Dudgeon began
investigating her childhood, uncovering a connection to playwright J. M. Barrie
(1860–1937). Barrie had learned the art of hypnosis, which he used to psychologically control the lives of du Maurier's family and that of her cousins, the
Davies, who were the models for the Lost Boys in Barrie's play *Peter Pan*. In
this investigative biography, Dudgeon portrays Barrie as a manipulator who
drove several of his victims to suicide.

Hibbert, Christopher
The Borgias and Their Enemies 1431–1519. 2008. Harcourt. 328p. ISBN
9780151010332.

When Spaniard Alfonso Borgia (1378–1458) moved to Naples in 1442 to become private secretary of King Alfonso V of Aragon, he set off a series of events
that led to his becoming Pope Calixtus III and gave his family a secure base from
which to seize power, wealth, and land. In this compelling family biography featuring corruption and murder, historian and novelist Christopher Hibbert recounts
the bloody lives of Alfonso, his nephew Rodrigo Borgia who became Pope Alexander VI, and Rodrigo's notoriously well-known children Cesare and Lucrezia.

Hodel, Steve
*Most Evil: Avenger, Zodiac, and the Further Serial Murders of Dr. George Hill
Hodel*. 2009. Dutton. 309p. ISBN 9780525951322.

In *Black Dahlia Avenger*, former Los Angeles Police Department detective Steve Hodel told an incredible story about discovering that his father was
a brutal murderer. In this sequel, the author presents his further discovery that
his father Dr. George Hill Hodel (1908–1999) was a serial killer who left unsolved murders in Chicago, Manila, and San Francisco. In this well-illustrated
documentary biography, a son reveals the life and character of a master criminal whose talent for escape kept him at large until his death at 91.

Leake, John

▶ *Entering Hades: The Double Life of a Serial Killer*. 2007. Farrar, Straus & Giroux. 350p. ISBN: 9780374148454.

Who truly knows when a criminal is rehabilitated? While in prison, Jack Unterweger (1950–1994) completed his education and became the successful author of an autobiography and children's stories. With many positive references, he was pardoned by an Austrian court after serving 14 years of a life sentence for murder. In this true crime biography, philosopher John Leake examines a man who doubled as a crime reporter and brutally killed at least six prostitutes within a year of his release.

Montefiore, Simon Sebag

Young Stalin. 2007. Alfred A. Knopf. 460p. ISBN 9781400044658.

Soviet Premier and Chairman of the Communist Party Joseph Stalin (1879–1953) has long been viewed in the West as a brutal dictator, but his origins were not well known. Using documents recently made public, historian Simon Sebag Montefiore discovered that as a youth, Stalin was a member of a notorious gang and guilty of many crimes, including bank robbery, arson, and murder. How a ruthless gangster became a top aide of Vladimir Ilyich Lenin is told in this investigative biography.

Reiterman, Tim

Raven: The Untold Story of the Rev. Jim Jones and His People. 1982. E. P. Dutton. 622p. ISBN 0525241361.

Journalist Tim Reiterman was investigating the Peoples Temple of the Rev. Jim Jones (1931–1978) when he and the party of Congressman Leo Ryan were ambushed at a small airport in Guyana. At that moment, Jones was back at the Temple compound leading the suicide of more than 900 followers. Reiterman survived to conduct hundreds of interviews and write this account that takes a look into the character of an idealistic but troubled man who as a boy had shot a friend with a BB gun just to witness his companion's reaction.

Short, Philip

Pol Pot: Anatomy of a Nightmare. 2004. Henry Holt and Company. 537p. ISBN 0805066624.

Secrecy was always required by Cambodian rebel leader Pol Pot (1925–1998), born Saloth Sâr, also known as Pouk, Hay, Grand-Uncle, and First Brother. Throughout the Communist uprising and until two years after the fall of Phnom Penh, the true identity of the central member of the Khmer Rouge was unknown to Cambodian officials, the CIA, and even most of his own followers. After more than 20 years of investigating Pol Pot and conducting interviews with many former Khmer Rouge militants, foreign correspondent Philip Short tells how an ideological teacher obsessed with utopia became the head executioner of a self-destructive revolution.

Standard Bearers

In biography, some lives are offered as models for the rest of us. Their stories are told to inspire us to be as determined as African American singer Marian Anderson when she was denied a stage, as courageous as Lou Gehrig when he faced a debilitating disease, or as loyal as Margaret Roper when her father Thomas More was condemned for opposing Henry VIII's marriage to Anne Boleyn. The following characters through words and actions encourage readers to be loyal, ethical, and brave.

Arsenault, Raymond
▶ *The Sound of Freedom: Marian Anderson, the Lincoln Memorial, and the Concert That Awakened America*. 2009. Bloomsbury. 310p. ISBN 9781596915787.

Singer Marian Anderson was as important a civil rights figure as boxer Joe Louis, baseball star Jackie Robinson, and seamstress Rosa Parks. With her beautiful voice and insistence on her right to be heard in the finest concert halls despite her race, she exposed the absurdity of Jim Crow laws prevalent from the 1920s to the 1950s. In this laudatory account of Anderson's career, Raymond Arsenault portrays the singer as a humble and somewhat shy person who never set out to be a hero.

Bundy, Carol
The Nature of Sacrifice: A Biography of Charles Russell Lowell, Jr., 1835–1864. 2005. Farrar, Straus and Giroux. 548p. ISBN 0374120773.

Killed in the Battle at Cedar Creek, General Charles Russell Lowell, Jr. (1835–1864) was returned to Boston for a magnificent funeral attended by his esteemed family and friends, including Ralph Waldo Emerson, Henry Wadsworth Longfellow, and Oliver Wendell Holmes. Young Lowell had been foreseen by abolitionist, blue-blooded Bostonians as a future industrialist and political leader, and his death was proclaimed an ultimate sacrifice for the cause of the Union. In this epic biography, film writer Carol Bundy recounts in detail the education and military career of a favorite son.

Claridge, Laura
Emily Post: Daughter of the Gilded Age, Mistress of American Manners. 2008. Random House. 525p. ISBN 9780375509216.

Who would imagine that the most revered judge of good behavior was once involved in a scandalous divorce? Socialite Emily Post (1872–1960) was stung badly by the infidelity of her husband and inspired to become an advocate for women. Emboldened to campaign for the respectful treatment of all people, she wrote a good manners guide that she called *Etiquette*. Biographer Laura Claridge recounts how Post encouraged many people to reform their lives through reverence and good conduct.

Eggers, Dave
Zeitoun. 2009. McSweeney's Books. 351p. ISBN 9781934781630. ☙ ♘
>   Painting contractor Abdulrahman Zeitoun of New Orleans was nearly a model citizen. As an immigrant from Syria, he had worked hard to build up his own business with dozens of employees and scores of loyal customers across the city. His only fault was not obeying the mayor's order to vacate the city in advance of Hurricane Katrina. With admiration, author Dave Eggers recounts the good deeds, bad fortune, and graceful recovery of an honest man wrongfully arrested as a terrorist.

Eig, Jonathan
Luckiest Man: The Life and Death of Lou Gehrig. 2005. Simon & Schuster. 420p. ISBN: 9780743245913.
>   New York Yankee first baseman Lou Gehrig (1903–1941) was born poor, but his mother worked hard to feed him and keep him in school. As a high school student, he was said to be clumsy and slow at sports, but his coaches let him develop into the strongest hitter in the school's history. As a remedial student on scholarship at Columbia University, he impressed major league scouts. In this inspiring biography, journalist Jonathan Eig portrays Gehrig as a solitary man who could easily have failed at nearly any point in his life but instead earned the respect of generations of baseball fans.

Gooch, Brad
Flannery: A Life of Flannery O'Connor. 2009. Little, Brown. 448p. ISBN 9780316000666.
>   Flannery O'Connor (1925–1964) claimed that her life spent between the house and the chicken yard in Milledgeville, Georgia, would never prompt the writing of a biography. Her letters to her many literary friends, however, still excite readers who enjoy sharp wit and spiritual ideas. Literary biographer Brad Gooch recounts O'Connor's determined effort to write startlingly original fiction and maintain her dignity while suffering from lupus erythematosus, from which she would die before her 40th birthday.

Guy, John
Daughter's Love: Thomas More and His Dearest Meg. 2009. Houghton Mifflin Harcourt. 378p. ISBN 9780618499151. ☙
>   When Sir Thomas More (1478–1535) was arrested for treason for opposing the marriage of Henry VIII to Anne Boleyn, only his daughter Margaret Roper (1505–1544) risked her own life by regularly visiting him in the Tower of London. Her loyalty to her father was unshaken by the grave danger of her being judged treasonous by association. After his execution, only she had the courage to ask for the return of his head. In this admiring dual biography, historian John Guy recounts the close relationship between the virtuous father and the daughter who preserved his letters and essays.

Maraniss, David

Clemente: The Passion and Grace of Baseball's Last Hero. 2006. Simon & Schuster. 401p. ISBN 9780743217811.

Pittsburgh Pirates outfield Roberto Clemente (1934–1972) was acclaimed as a genuinely well-rounded athlete, effective leader, and humanitarian. Having risen from poverty in Puerto Rico, he was well aware that he was a symbol for all Latin players and the people of his country and strove to deserve his fame. In this admiring biography, David Maraniss shows how Clemente took his responsibility so seriously that he risked and lost his life in service to people in need.

Chapter Two

Story

In the musical *Bye Bye Birdie*, all the teens want to know about their friends Hugo and Kim. Did they really get pinned? Where did it happen? Did he kiss her? Will it last? The boys in the locker room particularly want to know why Hugo did it. They want the full story.

We all enjoy good stories and seek them in libraries and bookstores. Story is the most advertised and compelling feature of most popular reading. While character might be the primary appeal for readers choosing biography, story would have to be a close second, and a good story is essential to keep readers reading about biographical subjects, such as the industrialist Andrew Carnegie. Was he really born poor? Who were his family? How did he make his fortune? Why did he feel the urge to give to charities? Did he die a happy man? We want the full story.

In this chapter are 16 book lists featuring biographies about people whose lives can be seen as particular types of stories, such as "Coming of Age," "Rags to Riches," or "True Crimes." The final three lists, "Trouble at Home," "Great Rivalries," and "Fragile Friendships," feature numerous dual, collective, and family biographies.

Coming of Age

The time of transition from being a youth to becoming a mature adult is often fraught with indecision and sometimes danger. Without understanding the consequences, youths must sometimes make choices that will forever shape their lives. Some, such as Jane Addams who founded Hull House, do well, but others, such as ingenue Evelyn Nesbit, falter. The literature of coming-of-age biographies is particularly rich. The following are just a few samples.

Allen, Charles
Kipling Sahib: India and the Making of Rudyard Kipling, 1865–1900. 2009. Pegasus Books. 426p. ISBN 9781605980317.

As the 19th century became the 20th, Rudyard Kipling (1865–1936) emerged as one of the most famous men in the world, a literary giant and an embodiment of the spirit of the British Empire. Magazines promised to print anything written by the acclaimed expert on India. In this sympathetic biography, British journalist Charles Allen recounts the happier half of the Kipling life, his childhood in Bombay and early years as an editor for the *Civil and Military Gazette* in Lahore before writing his 1900 novel *Kim*.

Diliberto, Gioia
▶ *A Useful Woman: The Early Life of Jane Addams*. 1999. Scribner. 318p. ISBN 06848536 55. ⬱

Before social activist Jane Addams (1860–1935) dedicated herself to the care of the poor, she was a reluctant debutante who found little joy in the high society into which she was born. She was not alone. Finding like-minded young women, she established Hull House, a mission house for women, children, and immigrants in Chicago. Gioia Diliberto chronicles the transformation of young Addams from an unhappy daughter of society into an American icon for charity in this admiring biography.

Heymann, C. David
American Legacy: The Story of John and Caroline Kennedy. 2007. Atria Books. 592p. ISBN 9780743497381.

How could the children of an assassinated president mature into well-adjusted adults ready to follow their parents into the national spotlight? For John Kennedy Jr. (1960–1999) and Caroline Kennedy (1957–), their mother's strategy was to keep them out of the public eye by sending them to exclusive schools and secluded estates. They eventually slipped her bonds. Author C. David Heymann reveals the brave but flawed individuals the siblings became in this melancholic dual biography.

Morris, Roy, Jr.
Lighting Out for the Territory: How Samuel Clemens Headed West and Became Mark Twain. 2010. Simon & Schuster. 282p. ISBN 9781416598664.

As the American Civil War began, Samuel Clemens's (1835–1910) rootless life as a riverboat pilot was disrupted, as both the Union and Confederate armies tried to draft him into their ranks. Disliking his odds of survival, he fled to Nevada. In this entertaining account that revises Clemens's unreliable memoir *Roughing It*, biographer Roy Morris Jr. shows how several years in the West transformed the purposeless young man into the popular author Mark Twain.

Reynolds, Michael

The Young Hemingway. 1986. Basil Blackwell. 291p. ISBN 0631147861.

In 1919, when Ernest Hemingway (1899–1961) returned to the United States from his service as an ambulance driver in World War I, the nation was mourning the death of the young man's hero, Theodore Roosevelt. As he returned to his quiet suburban home in Oak Park, Illinois, Hemingway dreamed of combining Roosevelt-like world travel and adventure with writing to win fame and fortune. For three years, he struggled to write something worthy of attention, before sailing to Europe with his new bride to find new inspiration. In this slice-of-life biography, literary scholar Michael Reynolds recounts the time during which Hemingway created a new identity.

Starkey, David

Elizabeth: The Struggle for the Throne. 2001. HarperCollins. 363p. ISBN 0060184973.

Before she became queen of England, Elizabeth I (1533–1603) lived precariously. After her mother Anne Boleyn was beheaded, she was banished from her father's court to live with a predatory foster father, and she was later imprisoned on suspicion of treason during the reign of her half-sister Mary. Once on the throne, she was the target of assassins and endangered by the discord among her advisors. In this suspenseful biography, historian David Starkey recounts how young Elizabeth quickly learned her role as monarch, won the hearts of her subjects, and took control of her government.

Thorpe, Helen

Just Like Us: The True Story of Four Mexican Girls Coming of Age in America. 2009. Scribner. 387p. ISBN 9781416538936. ☙

Four studious high school girls in Colorado seemed inseparable and of one mind until graduation, when their differing statuses as citizens, legal residents, and illegal aliens separated their fates. Investigative reporter Helen Thorpe joined the girls in their senior year and followed them through four years of college. Thorpe describes their struggles to find roles in the United States against the backdrop of the national immigration debate. This is a rare biography in which names have been changed to protect subjects from deportation.

Uruburu, Paula

American Eve: Evelyn Nesbit, Stanford White, the Birth of the "It" Girl, and the Crime of the Century. 2008. Riverhead Books. 386p. ISBN 9781594489938.

With no misgivings, young model Evelyn Nesbit (1884–1967) entered New York's world of fashion and entertainment at 16. After a few short years of flirting with handsome and powerful men, she married jealous millionaire Harry Thaw. After Thaw publicly murdered Nesbit's lover, the up-and-coming architect Stanford White, the young woman's riotous life was reported in newspapers across the country. In this somewhat sympathetic biography, author Paula Uruburu describes a young woman without scruples who learned too slowly how to be discreet.

Rags to Riches

In 19th-century America, stories of men who had seemingly risen from poverty to become fabulously wealthy captains of industry were highly popular, as readers of the time felt that such success stories modeled characters to emulate. The American desire for riches continues today, and biographies of self-made multimillionaires, such as Andrew Carnegie or Cornelius Vanderbilt, sell well alongside titles on investments and marketing. These eight modern biographies will attract readers who enjoy good rags-to-riches stories.

Berridge, Kate
Madame Tussaud: A Life in Wax. 2006. William Morrow. 352p. ISBN 9780060528478.

While many of her countrymen were losing their heads at the guillotine, Madame Tussaud (1761–1850) was turning a tidy profit by exhibiting grisly wax reenactments of daily events. Though the daughter of a simple cook, she discovered she had a knack for lurid entertainment that brought people of all classes to her museum. In this entertaining biography, Kate Berridge recounts the life of a legendary entertainment entrepreneur whose name is synonymous with creepy amusements.

Cohodas, Nadine
Spinning Blues into Gold: The Chess Brothers and the Legendary Chess Records. 2000. St. Martin's Press. 358p. ISBN 0312261330.

Brothers Leonard Chess (1917–1969) and Phil Chess (1921–) sold their first records out of the trunk of a car after a concert that they had promoted. As Polish immigrants growing up in Chicago's Jewish community, they learned well how to hustle for the extra dollar that would make a business succeed. In this frank but respectful biography, social historian Nadine Cohodas recounts how the brothers prospered by recording black musicians who were often ignored by the big record companies before and during the volatile years of the Civil Rights Movement.

D'Antonio, Michael
▶ *A Full Cup: Sir Thomas Lipton's Extraordinary Life and His Quest for the America's Cup*. 2010. Riverhead Books. 354p. ISBN 9781594487606.

Son of a box factory worker, tea magnate Thomas Lipton (1850–1931) began his career as an errand boy before becoming a shirt maker in Glasgow, Scotland. Then, by working as a cabin boy on a steamship, he crossed the Atlantic Ocean to America where he learned retail methods that he took back

to Scotland to start his own grocery. With P. T. Barnum–like flair for promotion and keen business sense, he transformed his store into the world's first
grocery chain and became a leading marketer of tea. In this entertaining biography, author Michael D'Antonio tells how the charming Lipton became
a folk hero for using his self-earned wealth to support charities and doggedly
pursuing America's most famous yachting title.

Dolan, Brian
Wedgwood: The First Tycoon. 2004. Viking. 396p. ISBN 0670033464.

Josiah Wedgwood (1730–1795) was just a potter's son, but he learned his
craft well and had an idea for improving ceramic glazes. Through experimen-
tation, he developed a brighter white that impressed business partners and a
growing population of consumers, including European monarchs. Admiring
biographer Brian Dolan tells how the inventive Wedgwood was able to build
an innovative ceramics factory and used his well-earned fortune to become a
leading British citizen and friend to eminent scientists of his time.

Fried, Stephen
*Appetite for America: How Visionary Businessman Fred Harvey Built a Rail-
road Hospitality Empire That Civilized the Wild West*. 2010. Bantam Books.
518p. ISBN 9780553804379.

After his father was found insolvent in a London bankruptcy court, eight-
year-old Fred Harvey (1835–1901) vowed to never be so humiliated. Ten years
later, with only two pounds in his wallet, he arrived in America and made
his way to St. Louis, where he learned the restaurant trade. By the end of the
century, he had established a network of hotels, restaurants, dining cars, gift
shops, and bookstores across the American West. In this admiring biography
of Harvey and his family, journalist Stephen Fried describes the lives of an innovative entrepreneur and the descendants who kept his company prosperous
for half a century after his death.

Jenkins, Carol, and Elizabeth Gardner Hines
Black Titan: A. G. Gaston and the Making of a Black Millionaire. 2004. One
World. 320p. ISBN 0345453476.

In the early 20th century, few coal miners ever escaped poverty. Miner
A. G. Gaston (1892–1996) did so by selling inexpensive lunches to his coworkers and using his profits to found a bank for miners. Having a knack for business,
he eventually started 10 companies, established charities, and became an advisor
to Presidents Kennedy and Johnson. Gaston's remarkable story is admiringly
told by Carol Jenkins and Elizabeth Gardner Hines, a niece and a daughter.

Nasaw, David
Andrew Carnegie. 2006. Penguin Press. 878p. ISBN 1594201048.

At 13, Scottish immigrant Andrew Carnegie (1835–1919) worked
12 hours a day as a bobbin boy in a Pennsylvania cotton mill for $2.00 a week.
By the time of his death, the industrialist was one of the world's richest men
and greatest philanthropists. Ironically, he fought bitterly against aspiring

laborers wanting raises. Author David Nasaw presents a balanced account of a complicated man whose generosity was as strong as his miserliness.

Stiles, T.J.
The First Tycoon: The Epic Life of Cornelius Vanderbilt. 2009. Alfred A. Knopf. 719p. ISBN 9780375415425. ȣ
Cornelius Vanderbilt (1794–1877) rose from the old Dutch of Staten Island, prosperous and hardworking people who were belittled by the cream of New York society. Vanderbilt, who began as a boatman ferrying passengers to Manhattan, built steamships, took over railroads, befriended presidents, and became the richest and most powerful man in the United States. In this epic biography, veteran historian T.J. Stiles recounts a life filled with commerce, conflict, and high society.

The Power of Business

In theory, money is simply a tool to help people exchange goods and services. In reality, individuals, such as publisher Henry Luce and banker Andrew W. Mellon, acquire and use vast amounts of capital to earn status, steer the economy, and elect government officials to their liking, which may or may not benefit society as a whole. The following biographies recount stories of ambitious individuals whose commercial transactions have created the modern business-oriented world.

Brinkley, Alan
The Publisher: Henry Luce and His American Century. 2010. Alfred A. Knopf. 531p. ISBN 9780679414445.
Born to American missionaries in rural China, magazine publisher Henry Luce (1898–1967) inherited the belief that his purpose was to change his world. As he saw it, his mission was to spread the American gospel of democracy and capitalism through the publishing of popular magazines, including *Time*, *Fortune*, and *Life*. In this detailed chronicle of Luce's life and career, historian Alan Brinkley shows how by hiring talented writers, courting politicians, and swaying public opinion through his magazines, the quiet but relentless businessman succeeded in shaping his times.

Cannadine, David
Mellon: An American Life. 2006. Alfred A. Knopf. 779p. ISBN 0679450327.
In the late 19th century, Pittsburgh was the birthplace of millionaires who shaped the American economy to compete and dominate world markets. Among the city's elite was Andrew W. Mellon (1855–1937), a risk-taking banker and industrialist who transformed a comfortable inheritance into an unbelievable wealth. Later, as a member of the Harding, Coolidge, and Hoover administrations, he is often credited with fostering the Roaring Twenties and causing the Great

Depression. Believing Mellon is unfairly vilified, historian David Cannadine recounts in full a life of business, public service, and philanthropy.

Cruikshank, Jeffrey L., and Arthur W. Schultz
The Man Who Sold America: The Amazing (But True!) Story of Albert D. Lasker and the Creation of the Advertising Century. 2010. Harvard Business Review Press. 435p. ISBN 9781591393085. ⧉

When Albert Lasker (1880–1952) joined the advertising firm Lord & Thomas in 1898, the firm boasted that it had the finest typesetting, important in the age of simple box ads run in newspapers. In the next 50 years, Lasker transformed the company and the entire advertising industry, introducing reason why advertising campaigns, consumer coupons, and direct-mail marketing research. He also helped elect presidents and became the main philanthropist behind the American Cancer Society and Planned Parenthood. In their admiring biography, authors Jeffrey L. Cruikshank and Arthur W. Schultz tell how Lasker shaped the American consumer-based economy.

Davis, Jeff
Rozelle: Czar of the NFL. 2008. McGraw Hill. 544p. ISBN 9780071471664.

When Pete Rozelle became commissioner of the National Football League in 1960, there were only 12 teams, and revenues were far behind Major League Baseball. He negotiated big contracts with the major television networks, merged his league with the American Football League, and created the Super Bowl and Monday Night Football, as well as put down serious challenges from the Players Association, rogue owner Al Davis, and start-up leagues. In this admiring biography, journalist Jeff Davis tells how the commissioner changed the businesses of both sports and television.

Gleason, Janet
▶ *Millionaire: The Philanderer, Gambler, and Duelist Who Invented Modern Finance*. 1999. Simon & Schuster. 303p. ISBN 0684872951.

Scottish banker and felon John Law (1671–1729) cut a fine figure in his powered wig and elegant suit, impressing ladies in both London and Paris. Unable to sway Queen Anne to adopt paper money, he took his idea to the bankrupt French court, where after adopting French citizenship, he was allowed to create a bank with his gambling fortune. In this concise and lively biography, author Janet Gleason recounts the life of an audacious financier whose innovations are the foundation of modern capitalism.

McDonald, Duff
Last Man Standing: The Ascent of Jamie Dimon and JPMorgan Chase. 2009. Simon & Schuster. 340p. ISBN 9781416599531.

At nine, Jamie Dimon (1956–) declared that he would make a fortune. After graduating from Harvard Business School, he quickly rose through the ranks of investment bankers by boldly orchestrating great profits and saving banks on the brink of failure. When many banks failed in 2008, his bank JPMorgan Chase stood out for its solidity. Business journalist Duff McDonald profiles a master of financial foresight in this admiring biography.

Schroeder, Alice
The Snowball: Warren Buffett and the Business of Life. 2008. Bantam Books. 960p. ISBN 9780553805093.

When Warren Buffett (1930–) was six, he discovered that selling soda pop door to door in Omaha was more profitable than selling packs of gum. Fascinated with numbers and loving to sell, he was quickly charting ways to see his capital grow. Seventy years later, although he has made billions of dollars in profit, he has the same keen ability to spot what will sell and what will not. Investment analyst and admirer Alice Schroeder repeats many stories told to her by Buffett, his family, and his business associates in this entertaining biography.

Slack, Charles
Hetty: The Genius and Madness of America's First Female Tycoon. 2004. Ecco. 258p. ISBN 006054256X.

When 19th-century Wall Street analysts claimed that women had no knack for investing, they had to acknowledge Hetty Green (1835–1916) as the exception. As the daughter of a New Bedford shipping magnate, she amassed a fortune in real estate and railroad stocks during the heyday of robber barons Gould, Morgan, and Rockefeller. Called the Witch of Wall Street for being miserly and hard-hearted, Green was sometimes vilified for not being ladylike. In this quick-read biography, Charles Slack shows that Green could be both as generous and as ruthless as her rivals.

Fighting for Rights

The struggle for freedom is a theme that always resonates with people who have a belief in the sanctity of human rights. Readers respond with admiration for characters who like Moses lead their followers out of oppression. For their courage to demand rights, the stories of fighters, such as suffragist Elizabeth Cady Stanton and civil rights lawyer Thurgood Marshall, are remembered long after their lives. The following biographies feature stories of brave men or women working for the rights of oppressed people.

Biddle, Daniel R., and Murray Dubin
Tasting Freedom: Octavius Catto and the Battle for Equality in Civil War America. 2010. Temple University Press. 616p. ISBN 9781592134656.

African American Octavius Catto (1839–1871) was born free in Charleston, South Carolina, but enjoyed little liberty even when he moved to Philadelphia, the Quaker's City of Brotherly Love. Though he was acclaimed as a teacher, orator, and baseball player, he was relegated to black churches, schools, and transportation. In their detailed biography, Daniel R. Biddle and Murray Dubin recount the life of an outspoken black activist murdered by a white supremacist in the Election Day Riots of 1871.

Bradburd, Rus

Forty Minutes of Hell: The Extraordinary Life of Nolan Richardson. 2010. Amistad. 317p. ISBN 9780061690464.

Basketball coach Nolan Richardson (1941–) has confronted racial barriers all his life. When he was a popular college basketball player in El Paso in 1962, he asked for a soft drink in a whites-only restaurant and helped bring down local Jim Crow laws. Forty years later, after leading the University of Arkansas basketball team to an NCAA championship, Richardson publicly denounced the college basketball establishment for its reluctance to hire black coaches. In this sympathetic biography, author Rus Bradburd examines the life and career of a man fired for being candid about the state of racial relations in college sports.

Bryant, Howard

The Last Hero: A Life of Henry Aaron. 2010. Pantheon Books. 600p. ISBN 9780375424854.

Baseball star Henry Aaron (1934–) has been justly recognized for his athletic achievements, but his civil rights accomplishments are nearly forgotten. He coolly integrated the southern-based Sally League in the early 1950s and helped break regional racial barriers when the Braves moved to Atlanta in 1966, becoming the first major league team in the Deep South. While striving to surpass Babe Ruth's career home run record in 1974, he quietly endured constant threats from avowed racists. In this detailed psychological biography, sports correspondent Howard Bryant examines the enduring character of a man who still champions racial equality.

Chong, Denise

Egg on Mao: The Story of an Ordinary Man Who Defaced an Icon and Unmasked a Dictatorship. 2009. Counterpoint. 249p. ISBN 9781582435473.

Though born and raised in Mao Zedong's province of Hunan, Lu Decheng (1963–) grew to despise the veneration of the late Communist leader, who he realized was a cruel dictator. His father, employer, teachers, and neighbors chided him for disrespect, warning him of dire consequences if he continued to be outspoken. When Chinese students demanding democracy gathered on Tiananmen Square in 1989, he had to be there. Biographer Denise Chong recounts how a defiant man, who shocked his comrades by throwing paint-filled eggs at the portrait of Mao, withstood many years in a Chinese prison.

Ginzberg, Lori D.

Elizabeth Cady Stanton: An American Life. 2009. Hill and Wang. 254p. ISBN 9780809094936.

To suffragist Elizabeth Cady Stanton (1815–1902), it was self-evident that she was as capable of understanding public policy and voting as any man.

While on the surface she was a conventional wife and mother, the quick-witted Stanton enjoyed sparking fierce debates and making radical statements that were printed in newspapers across the country. In this quick-read biography, historian Lori D. Ginzberg presents Stanton as a founder and philosophical force behind the American Women's Rights Movement.

James, Rawn, Jr.

▶ *Root and Branch: Charles Hamilton Houston, Thurgood Marshall, and the Struggle to End Segregation.* 2010. Bloomsbury. 276p. ISBN 9781596916067.

When Howard University law professor Charles Hamilton Houston (1895–1950) was asked to defend a black man accused of murder in Virginia in 1933, he insisted on including his third-year student Thurgood Marshall (1908–1993) on his team. Though it was a hopeless case, it marked the beginning of their partnership targeting Jim Crow laws in labor, housing, and education. In this admiring dual biography, attorney Rawn James Jr. recounts how Marshall stepped up after Houston's early death to successfully argue for school desegregation in the landmark case *Brown v. Board of Education.*

Metaxas, Eric

Bonhoeffer: Pastor, Martyr, Prophet, Spy: A Righteous Gentile vs. the Third Reich. 2010. Thomas Nelson. 591p. ISBN 9781595551382. ☙

As an outspoken theologian, Dietrich Bonhoeffer (1906–1945) was a high-profile opponent of Adolf Hitler and his Nazi regime. This best-selling Lutheran author had admonished his church for capitulating to Nazi demands to condemn Jews and worked with conspirators planning to overthrow the führer. He even returned to Germany in 1939 to be a part of the resistance, a cause for which he died. In this epic biography, author Eric Metaxas recounts the passionate life and dangerous work of a modern martyr.

Newman, Richard S.

Freedom's Prophet: Bishop Richard Allen, the AME Church, and the Black Founding Fathers. 2008. New York University Press. 359p. ISBN 9780814758267.

When the writers of the U.S. Constitution failed to outlaw slavery, religious leaders began a campaign to rectify the omission. Among them was former slave and pamphlet writer Richard Allen (1760–1831), known as the Apostle of Freedom, a passionate Methodist who had earned his freedom before he was 20. He founded the African Methodist Episcopal Church and the Free African Society, the first organization created in the abolition movement. Historian Richard S. Newman pays tribute to an eloquent speaker, early advocate of nonviolent protest, and smart businessman in this inspiring biography.

Lives on Trial

Television producers have long known that courtroom proceedings can make dramatic viewing. From *Perry Mason* to *Law and Order*, scriptwriters have cast lawyers, defendants, and witnesses in stories that need juries to resolve. Biographers have also used court testimony and out-of-court maneuvering to add tension to their narratives, including stories of Greek philosopher Socrates, astronomer Galileo, and boxer Rubin Carter. The following list includes eight biographies weaving courtroom scenes into their stories.

Dillon, Patrick, and Carl M. Cannon
   Circle of Greed: The Spectacular Rise and Fall of the Lawyer That Brought Corporate America to Its Knees. 2010. Broadway Books. 532p. ISBN 9780767929943.

   Successfully suing powerful corporations to expose and punish them for their corrupt practices, lawyer William S. Lerach (1946–) became rich and famous. Lerach especially enjoyed prying millions of dollars from companies such as Disney, CitiBank, Arthur Anderson, and Enron, but to maintain his success in court and protect profits, he resorted to fraud and kickback schemes. In this detailed investigative biography, journalists Patrick Dillon and Carl M. Cannon recount the dramatic career of a Robin Hood–like hero who became as greedy as his enemies.

Ekirch, A. Roger
   Birthright: The True Story That Inspired Kidnapped. 2010. W. W. Norton. 258p. ISBN 9780393066159.

   James Annesley (1715–1760) was the son of Arthur Annesley, baron of Altham, and thus heir to his father's lands and titles in both Ireland and England. Unfortunately for James, his father was a drunkard and wastrel, who let his second wife send James away to live as a pauper. When his father died, James was kidnapped by his uncle, who was next in line to inherit, and sold into indentured servitude in the American colonies. When after more than 10 years he returned to Great Britain, he sued to establish his identity and claim his inheritance. In this historical biography, A. Roger Ekirch recounts a series of sensational trials that later inspired novels by Robert Louis Stevenson and Sir Walter Scott.

Hirsch, James S.
   Hurricane: The Miraculous Journey of Rubin Carter. 2000. Houghton Mifflin. 358p. ISBN 0395979854.

   The 1967 murder conviction of black boxer Rubin "Hurricane" Carter (1937–) by an all-white jury drew the attention of civil rights groups and celebrities, who suspected that New Jersey prosecutors manufactured the evidence.

For 22 years, Carter and his allies fought in court for his release from death row and exoneration. In this candid biography of a street tough transformed into a folk hero, author James S. Hirsch recounts the legal maneuvering that set Rubin Carter free.

Hofstadter, Dan

The Earth Moves: Galileo and the Roman Inquisition. 2009. W.W. Norton. 240p. ISBN 9780393066500.

In many accounts of the 1,632 papal proceedings against Galileo Galilei, the astronomer/mathematician/philosopher is cast as a defender of science and truth, and Pope Urban VIII is vilified as a backward church father, unwilling to face modernity. In these books, Galileo insists the sun is the center of our part of the universe, whereas the pope retains the belief in the earth as the center of creation. Dan Hofstadter shows the case was a bit more complicated, the pope more astute, and Galileo less noble in this quick-read portrait of one of the most famous Renaissance thinkers.

Larson, Kate Clifford

The Assassin's Accomplice: Mary Surratt and the Plot to Kill Abraham Lincoln. 2008. Basic Books. 263p. ISBN 9780465038152. ☙

Justice was swift in 1865. Within three months of the assassination of President Abraham Lincoln, four conspirators were hung, among them innkeeper Mary Surratt (1823–1865). Although the newspapers had vilified her, many people thought her role did not merit her punishment. In this lively account, historian Kate Clifford Larson carefully reexamines the woman and her trial to assess her guilt.

McRae, Donald

▶ ***The Last Trials of Clarence Darrow.*** 2009. William Marrow. 422p. ISBN 9780061161490.

After a decade recovering from a charge of jury tampering, legendary defense attorney Clarence Darrow (1857–1938) regained his stride in the 1920s in three front-page court trials. In defending first the notorious thrill killers Leopold and Loeb, then a teacher who incorporated the theory of evolution in his science class, and finally a black doctor charged with murder for protecting his house from a white mob, the persuasive attorney restored his fame and reputation. In this slice-of-life biography, author Donald McRae embeds these courtroom stories within an account of Darrow's declining career and failing marriage.

Spoto, Donald

Joan: The Mysterious Life of the Heretic Who Became a Saint. 2007. Harper-SanFrancisco. 220p. ISBN 9780060815172.

Nearly 600 years ago, a young French woman named Jeanne was tried by the Roman Catholic Church for heresy. Because the court transcripts survive, we know much about the short but dramatic life of the woman now known as Joan of Arc (1412–1431). In this sympathetic account, biographer Donald Spoto mixes court testimony with Jeanne's letters and the journals from her contemporaries to defend her role in history.

Waterfield, Robin
Why Socrates Died: Dispelling the Myths. 2009. W.W. Norton. 253p. ISBN 9780393065275.

Socrates left no writings, but more is known about the Greek philosopher than any other Athenian citizen of his time, according to author Robin Waterfield. His students Plato and Xenophon left detailed accounts of his teachings, and several Greek dramatists commented on his ideas in their plays. Combining these philosophical works with other Greek sources, Waterfield deftly recounts the life of an unorthodox citizen whose politics disturbed a jury of his contemporaries enough that they condemned him to death.

True Crimes

True crime stories have long been the staple of newspapers, magazines, and books. Readers want to know not only what happened but also what motivated the criminals. Why did mobster Baby Face Nelson kill, pickpocket George Appo steal, and firefighter John Orr set fires? Because readers often find criminals more interesting than the good people they harm, the following books should be popular.

Brock, Pope
Charlatan: America's Most Dangerous Huckster, the Man Who Pursued Him, and the Age of Flimflam. 2008. Crown Publishers. 324p. ISBN 9780307339881.

The American public has always fallen for smooth and folksy characters, such as patent medicine huckster John R. Brinkley (1885–1942). With his radio show and clinic in Kansas, he made a fortune promising hair replacement, virility, and longevity. Though the American Medical Association countered his claims regularly, Brinkley prospered and almost became governor of his state. Journalist Pope Brock recounts the life of an outrageous character who made crime pay.

Carlo, Philip
Gaspipe: Confessions of a Mafia Boss. 2008. William Morrow. 346p. ISBN 9780061429842.

Anthony Casso (1942–) was groomed by his father to be a Mafia kingpin. Michael Casso took Anthony to South Brooklyn's social clubs when he was 9 to learn how deals were made by men of respect, and at 12 the obedient son observed the murder of gangster Joe Monosco. Casso learned his lessons well and prospered as a dealer in drugs and murder. Trusted by Casso to tell his story fairly, childhood neighbor Philip Carlo recounts the candid confessions of the imprisoned killer.

Gilfoyle, Timothy J.

▶ *A Pickpocket's Tale: The Underworld of Nineteenth Century New York*. 2006. W. W. Norton. 460p. ISBN 9780393061901.

Just like Oliver Twist, George Appo (1856–1930) was an orphan living on the streets who joined a pickpocket gang. In his case, the city was mid-19th-century New York, and no benefactor saved him from his fate. He was arrested frequently and became such a local legend that he wrote a successful memoir and appeared in vaudeville reviews. In this gritty biography, historian Timothy J. Gilfoyle describes the life of a petty criminal who survived in a dangerous city.

James, Laura

The Love Pirate and the Bandit's Son: Murder, Sin, and Scandal in the Shadow of Jesse James. 2009. Union Square Press. 307p. ISBN 9781402760693.

When Zeo Zoe Wilkins (1885–1924) was brutally murdered, the Kansas City newspapers almost cheered. Known for her shady medical practice and a string of divorces, the beautiful woman with an ill-gotten fortune was not going to be missed. Jesse James Jr. (1876–1951), son of the famous outlaw, was one of her lawyers. In this lively dual biography of ruthless characters, crime historian Laura James (no relation to the outlaw) reveals that Wilkins and James had a criminal relationship that turned deadly.

Nickel, Steven, and William J. Helmer

Baby Face Nelson: Portrait of a Public Enemy. 2002. Cumberland House. 402p. ISBN 1581822723.

Make no mistake—Lester Joseph Gillis (1903–1934) was a hardened criminal. Much of what J. Edgar Hoover and his agents from the FBI reported about this outlaw, known to the public as Baby Face Nelson, however, was exaggeration. Crime historians Steven Nickel and William J. Helmer dispel the image of Baby Face as the nation's most bloodthirsty killer and portray him as a well-networked criminal who carefully planned a decade of crime.

O'Faolain, Nuala

The Story of Chicago May. 2005. Riverhead Books. 307p. ISBN 1573223204. ☙

Mary Ann Duignan (1871–1929) never apologized for stealing her father's savings to escape Ireland. In her memoir, the once-beautiful young woman blamed her father for refusing her the money, which she spent emigrating to Nebraska, where she began a career of crime and prostitution that later took her to Chicago, New York, Paris, and finally Detroit. Though previous books have portrayed the woman known as Chicago May as evil, author Nuala O'Faolain reconsiders her subject in light of Duignan's desperate circumstances.

Partnoy, Frank
The Match King: Ivar Kreuger, the Financial Genius behind a Century of Wall Street Scandals. 2009. Public Affairs. 272p. ISBN 9781586487430.

Early in the 20th century, safety matches were used countless times daily in most modern homes. Charismatic Swedish businessman Ivar Kreuger (1880–1932) built an international corporation founded on government-granted monopolies to sell the humble match in a variety of European countries. Through the 1920s and even after the Crash of 1929, Kreuger earned hard-to-believe profits, which were exposed as fraudulent after his suicide. Wall Street historian Frank Partnoy tells a suspenseful story about a shady industrialist who discovered effective means to juggle the books.

Wambaugh, Joseph
Fire Lover: A True Story. 2002. William Morrow. 338p. ISBN 006009527X.

Glendale fire investigator John Orr (1949–) enjoyed catching arsonists and was admired across California for teaching firefighting and investigative skills. As a leader in his profession, it seemed natural that he might write a novel about arson, a subject that he knew well. No one suspected Orr of setting fires that killed four people. In this startling biography, best-selling novelist and former policeman Joseph Wambaugh recounts how after Glendale fire investigators discovered clues to unsolved cases in their friend's novel, Orr was arrested and convicted.

Down but Not Out

First you are up and then you are down. Can you get up again? Boxers get a count of 10, after which the match is over, but in the game of life, individuals may have more time to reestablish themselves after setbacks. Actress and singer Leona Horne lost roles due to aging and racial discrimination but continued to resurface on stage and screen throughout her career. Both England's Charles II and France's Marie-Thérèse survived their parents' beheadings and years of exile to return to power. The following stories about tenacious people come from the worlds of music, literature, politics, and science.

Coleman, Rick
Blue Monday: Fats Domino and the Lost Dawn of Rock and Roll. 2006. Da Capo Press. 364p. ISBN 9780306814914.

When the Beatles were in New Orleans in 1965, they sought out Fats Domino, the local rhythm and blues singer, a pioneer of rock and roll. It was almost a final highlight for a man whose career was on the wane. Indeed, when Domino was rescued during Hurricane Katrina in 2005, many fans were stunned to learn that the singer was still alive. In this loving tribute and candid account, rock historian Rick Coleman describes the up-and-down career of a key figure in the evolution of an American musical tradition.

Coots, Stephen
Royal Survivor: A Life of Charles II. 2000. St. Martins Press. 396p. ISBN 031222687x.

The life of Charles II of England (1630–1685) might have ended when his father Charles I was beheaded had he not been abroad. When the son's army of Scottish supporters was defeated at the Battle of Worcester, he escaped capture in the guise of a commoner. After years of poverty and conspiracy in exile on the continent, he was invited back to England to be king in 1660. In his intimate biography of Charles II, Stephen Coots recounts how once on the throne the Roman Catholic king slyly kept his crown despite being surrounded by Protestants eager to end the monarchy forever.

Gavin, James
Stormy Weather: The Life of Lena Horne. 2009. Atria Books. 598p. ISBN 9780743271431.

In 1994, when celebrity journalist James Gavin first met glamorous African American singer and actress Lena Horne (1917–2010), he found her bitter about how racial discrimination had limited her career. Despite beauty and talent, she had lost many roles deemed inappropriate for blacks. Yet, in her late 70s, Horne was releasing a new album and doing concerts to resurrect her career. In this sympathetic remembrance of a tenacious woman, Gavin recounts setbacks and rebounds of the first black actress to land romantic roles in Hollywood.

Merrill, Hugh
The Red Hot Typewriter: The Life and Times of John D. MacDonald. 2000. Thomas Dunne Books. 256p. ISBN 0312209053.

The path to becoming a successful author of hard-boiled detective stories was difficult for John D. MacDonald (1916–1986). Though he aspired to write great literature, his father insisted that he attend college and train to be a businessman. MacDonald lost or quit many jobs before finding some stability as a soldier in World War II. After the war, he moved his family to cheap accommodations in Florida and started to write. In this admiring biography, journalist Hugh Merrill chronicles MacDonald's difficult years of writing stories for mystery magazines and the paperback market before his ultimate success writing the Travis McGee stories.

Nagel, Susan
Marie-Therese, Child of Terror: The Fate of Marie Antoinette's Daughter. 2008. Bloomsbury. 418p. ISBN 9781596910577.

A crowd of French subjects gathered round the royal bed to witness the birth of Marie-Thérèse-Charlotte of France (1778–1851). So began a long public life once interrupted by imprisonment and twice by exile. Surviving the execution of her parents Louis XVI and Marie Antoinette, Marie-Therese later rose as an opponent of Napoleon Bonaparte. Against a backdrop of ever-changing French politics, biographer Susan Nagel recounts the perilous life of an astute woman who remained a prominent figure in French society and politics for more than a half century.

Nasar, Sylvia
▶ *A Beautiful Mind: A Biography of John Forbes Nash, Jr., Winner of the Nobel Prize in Economics, 1994*. 1998. Simon & Schuster. 459p. ISBN 0684819066. ⛉

Mathematician John Forbes Nash Jr. (1928–) has the gift of nonrational intuition, letting him see solutions to complex problems in the fields of game theory, computer architecture, and geometry in a flash. Unfortunately, for 30 years, the schizophrenic professor also saw extraterrestrials and felt that he had a messianic mission. In this sympathetic and admiring biography, economics reporter Sylvia Nasar chronicles how Nash recovered his cognitive abilities and won a Nobel Prize in Economics.

Rayfield, Donald
Anton Chekhov: A Life. 1997. Henry Holt. 674p. ISBN 0805057471.

Son of a Russian grocer living in dreary Taganrog, frozen in winter and boiling in summer, playwright and short story writer Anton Chekhov (1860–1904) knew hardship and tragedy. His father was abusive, his older brothers were drunkards, and tuberculosis killed aunts and uncles. Abandoned when his father went bankrupt, Chekhov worked odd jobs to pay his school fees, qualified to practice medicine, and began submitting stories to magazines to earn extra cash. Having studied newly available letters, Russian literature scholar Donald Rayfield tells how Chekhov continued to write inventive stories and plays through the hardest times.

Reisen, Harriet
Louisa May Alcott: The Woman behind Little Women. 2009. Henry Holt. 362p. ISBN 9780805082999. ⬱

The fictional March family in *Little Women* was never as poor and desperate as the real Alcotts were during the childhood and adolescence of Louisa May Alcott (1832–1888). With her industrious mother as a model and her father as a burden, Alcott worked any job that she could to keep the family fed, always dreaming of a fortune to come through writing. In this biography that unmasks Alcott's pulp fiction pen names, screenwriter Harriet Reisen reveals that even after publishing her fabulously popular books, Alcott repeatedly had to take up her pen to support the household despite her own bad health.

Smith, Richard D.
Can't You Hear Me Callin: The Life of Bill Monroe, Father of Bluegrass. 2000. Little, Brown and Company. 365p. ISBN 0316803812.

Born cross-eyed on Friday the 13th, the eighth son of a poor Kentucky farmer, Bill Monroe (1911–1996) knew hard times and how to sing about them. After creating the bluegrass sound with his roving band of hillbilly musicians, the talented mandolin player starred at the Grand Ole Opry for nearly 60 years.

According to music journalist Richard D. Smith, fame did not bring happiness, as Monroe lost band members Flatt and Scruggs in a bitter dispute and broke up with numerous wives and girlfriends. Smith portrays the lonesome Father of Bluegrass as often down but never out, a man who demanded respect more than love.

Sports Challenges

Sports may be a metaphoric device for the telling of any kind of story, but for some readers, it is the key attraction in the books they seek. They enjoy the drama that the reporting of athletic conditioning and contests of skill adds to sports biography. They may also be attracted to the statistical details of batting averages, free shots made, or passes completed. A character that can compete at the highest level is of particular interest to them, even when the story then ventures away from the field of play. The following biographies retell the stories of athletes whose actions changed their sports.

Anderson, Lars
The First Star: Red Grange and the Barnstorming Tout That Launched the NFL. 2009. Random House. 252p. ISBN 9781400067299.

Like other National Football League owners, Chicago Bears' owner and coach George Halas was losing money in the early 1920s. More than 20 teams in the new professional league had already folded. To the rescue came University of Illinois halfback Red Grange (1903–1991), a young man eager to score touchdowns and win the hearts of fans. In this career-focused biography, *Sports Illustrated* writer Lars Anderson tells how the astute Grange developed as both player and sports icon.

Belth, Alex
Stepping Up: The Story of Curt Flood and His Fight for Players' Rights. 2006. Persea Books. 228p. ISBN 0892553219.

Major League Baseball players earn huge salaries now, but when outfield Curt Flood (1938–1997) was involuntarily traded from the St. Louis Cardinals to the Philadelphia Phillies in 1969, players played for whatever they were offered. By walking off the field and suing team owners, Flood rebelled against the long-established rules that bound players to teams. He lost both the court case and his career. Sports journalist Alex Belth tells the courageous story of a man whose sacrifice ignited the players' union movement.

Callahan, Tom
Johnny U: The Life and Times of Johnny Unitas. 2006. Crown. 292p. ISBN 9781400081394.

Baltimore Colts Johnny Unitas (1933–2002) was an all-pro quarterback who led a hard-hitting team in an industrial city when professional football players identified with factory workers and dockhands. As an off-season construction worker and later as a bar owner, he was a symbol for the strength of the working class at a time when management had to listen to labor. In this admiring biography, sportswriter Tom Callahan recalls a time when quarterbacks—not committees of coaches looking down from skyboxes—called the plays on the football field.

Dodson, James
Ben Hogan: An American Life. 2004. Doubleday. 528p. ISBN 0385503121.

Before the era of Arnold Palmer and Jack Nicholas, Ben Hogan (1912–1977) was golf's most celebrated player. Having begun as a caddy, Hogan struggled with self-doubt and was well into his career before he began winning major professional tournaments. He also had to overcome career-threatening injuries from an automobile accident. In this admiring biography, famed golf journalist James Dodson recalls the life of a golf icon for a new generation of readers.

Larmer, Brooks
Operation Yao Ming: The Chinese Sports Empire, American Big Business, and the Making of an NBA Superstar. 2005. Gotham Books. 350p. ISBN 0151002967. ⇋

Eleven pounds at birth, Chinese basketball star Yao Ming (1980–) was literally born and raised to play basketball. His parents were the tallest couple in China, and Communist sports authorities began his training early. After dominating Chinese teams and playing brilliantly in the 2000 Olympics, he signed to play for the Houston Rockets. In this investigative report, journalist Brooks Larmer examines how Yao survived the pressure of Communist Party expectations to become a favorite player of fans around the world.

Lazenby, Roland
Jerry West: The Life and Legend of a Basketball Icon. 2009. Ballantine Books. 422p. ISBN 9780345510839.

As a West Virginia native and star for the West Virginia University Mountaineers, basketball's Jerry West (1938–) followed in the footsteps of the state's beloved player Hot Rod Hundley. As a player for the Los Angeles Lakers, he surpassed his role model, becoming one of the game's legends. Though immensely talented, the teams that he led as a player, coach, and general manager often failed to win championship games. In this detailed account of West's career, sports journalist Roland Lazenby examines a man whose intense style of play changed pro basketball.

Remnick, David
▶ *King of the World: Muhammad Ali and the Rise of an American Hero*. 1998. Random House. 326p. ISBN 0375500650. ☿

Boxer Muhammad Ali (1942–) has not always been an American fan favorite. Born Cassius Clay, he impressed the boxing world with his medal in the 1960

Olympics, but he was not thought to be a threat to top contenders Floyd Patterson and Sonny Liston when he became a professional that year. Backing brash talk with lightning-fast punching, Clay surprisingly earned the heavyweight championship and unveiled his shocking new name. In this lively sports biography, journalist David Remnick profiles Ali against a backdrop of sports and civil unrest.

Rosenfeld, Harvey
Iron Man: The Cal Ripkin, Jr., Story. 1995. St. Martin's Press. 276p. ISBN 0312135246.

With his father a catcher in the Oriole farm system and having been born in a Baltimore suburb, Cal Ripkin Jr. (1960–) seemed destined to be an Oriole shortstop. At 22, he was in the major leagues, won the American League Rookie of the Year Award, and started playing every Oriole game every season. When sports journalist Harvey Rosenfeld wrote this celebratory biography, Ripkin was on the verge of setting baseball's consecutive game endurance record. It is still a compelling account of the life of a player who won the admiration of teammates and fans nationwide.

Saving the Earth

Save the trees, the mountains, the wild horse, and the colorful birds. Save places for our children and grandchildren to enjoy nature. Save our own health and peace of mind. These are common pleas of the environmental movement that arose in the late 19th century when John Muir formed the Sierra Club and intensified when Rachel Carson wrote her influential book *Silent Spring*. The following list includes stories about Muir, Carson, and other people challenging society to save the earth.

Barcott, Bruce
The Last Flight of the Scarlet Macaw: One Woman's Fight to Save the World's Most Beautiful Bird. 2008. Random House. 313p. ISBN 9781400062935.

Director of the Belize Zoo Sharon Matola (1954–) learned in 1999 that the government of Belize was working with international energy company Fortis to build the Chalillo Dam, which would flood the valley home of the last of the country's scarlet macaws. The former Iowa housewife and lion tamer objected and quickly launched a campaign that led to threats to her safety and the future of the beloved zoo. Investigative reporter Bruce Barcott portrays Matola as a resourceful and courageous conservationist in this contemporary biography.

Brinkley, Douglas
Wilderness Warrior: Theodore Roosevelt and the Crusade for America. 2009. HarperCollins. 940p. ISBN 9780060565282.

Theodore Roosevelt (1858–1919) is a subject worthy of many biographies focusing on his different personas. Historian and talented storyteller Douglas Brinkley admiringly portrays the naturalist Roosevelt in this epic biography that recounts the subject's environmental education, career of advocacy, and world travel. Readers will especially enjoy learning how Roosevelt created the U.S. system of national parks, saving many just in the nick of time.

Cruise, David, and Alison Griffiths
Wild Horse Annie and the Last of the Mustangs: The Life of Velma Johnston. 2010. Scribner. 308p. ISBN 9781416553359.

When children's novelist Marguerite Henry wrote about Nevada wild horse advocate Velma Johnston (1912–1977), she naturally sanitized the story. The real Johnston drank heavily to ease the lasting pain of childhood polio that had left her disfigured, and raised among cowboys, she became a tough-speaking individual. In their biography that reads like a novel, authors David Cruise and Alison Griffiths tell how Johnston won her fight against ranchers and the Bureau of Land Management to stop the annual slaughter of wild horses on public lands.

Ehrlich, Gretel
John Muir: Nature's Visionary. 2000. National Geographic. 240p. ISBN 0792279549.

Young John Muir (1838–1914) was a wanderer and a truant before he found Yosemite. From the time he worked as a laborer in the park until his death, he spent much of his life outdoors, examining rocks, plants, and wildlife, and writing about his love of nature. In the process, he met kings and presidents. In this attractively illustrated biography, poet Gretel Ehrlich tracks the first president of the Sierra Club through the woods and mountains of California and on voyages around the world.

Furmansky, Dyana
Rosalie Edge, Hawk of Mercy: The Activist Who Saved Nature from the Conservationists. 2009. University of Georgia Press. 312p. ISBN 9780820333410.

Having been a prominent suffragist, New York socialite Rosalie Edge (1877–1962) knew firsthand how men of industry and politics enjoyed ridiculing women for their feminine causes. She also knew how some good men of conservation with fine ideals went along to get along with their business friends. The aptly named Edge, however, did not care about being polite and spoke for a more radical conservation movement in the 1920s to the 1940s, a time when environmental organizations had become clubs for the elite. Using Edge's personal papers and interviews with family, author Dyana Furmansky profiles a woman who paved the way for future environmental activists.

Humes, Edward
Eco Barons: The Dreamers, Schemers, and Millionaires Who Are Saving Our Planet. 2009. Ecco. 367p. ISBN 9780061350290. ☙

Having rich people turn private lands into wilderness does not always please people who reside in areas where they earn their income from industries that exploit nonrenewable resources. Millionaires Doug Tompkins and Ted

Turner in particular seem to have upset many people with secretive purchases and sudden announcements that their lands were closed to mining, lumbering, hunting, fishing, off-road vehicles, and development. Edward Humes tells about these and other eco barons in very readable profiles focusing on their methods and motivations.

Lorbiecki, Marybeth
Aldo Leopold: A Fierce Green Fire. 1996. Falcon Publishing. 212p. ISBN 1560444789.

Known for his nature classic *A Sand County Almanac*, Aldo Leopold (1886–1948) began his career as a forest ranger for the U.S. Forest Service at the time when the service favored the use of public lands by lumber and agricultural industries. Continually speaking out for the protection of wildlife earned him respect in the environmental community but resulted in exile to remote ranger stations. In this beautifully illustrated book, Marybeth Lorbiecki tells how Leopold became a noted author and champion of conservation.

Lytle, Mark Hamilton
▶ *The Gentle Subversive: Rachel Carson, Silent Spring, and the Rise of the Environmental Movement*. 2007. Oxford University Press. 277p. ISBN 9780195172461.

Before biologist Rachel Carson (1907–1964) spoke up, the use of the insecticide DDT on crops was touted by the government and the agricultural industry as an essential element of the Green Revolution to feed people around the world. Carson, however, found that the chemical was collecting in the tissues of birds, fish, and humans, leading to illness and birth defects. In this inspiring biography, Mark Hamilton Lytle describes how Carson sparked the environmental movement by writing her exposé *Silent Spring*.

Legends Examined

Did Buddha really live? When was Florence Nightingale a nurse? Why do we refer to Sarah Bernhardt tears? Many of us know their names but not their stories, which have been obscured by time and fictional accounts. For the following biographies, the authors have examined historical sources to sort fact from fiction and write modern accounts of legendary figures.

Armstrong, Karen
▶ *Buddha*. 2001. Lipper/Viking. 205p. ISBN 0670891932.

In religious author Karen Armstrong's compact book about Gotama Buddha (563?–483? BCE), ancient India was a curiously contemporary nation. Political corruption, financial stress, and urbanization sparked a longing among its people for a return to traditional values. It was also a place where the words of an ascetic were quickly reported. Drawing from legends and historical sources, Armstrong portrays the Buddha as a spiritual figure who captured the imagination of his troubled time.

Bostridge, Mark
Florence Nightingale: The Making of an Icon. 2008. Farrar, Straus and Giroux. 645p. ISBN 9780374156657.

British aristocrat turned battlefield nurse Florence Nightingale (1820–1910) is merely a symbol of compassion for most modern readers. Few know that after the mostly forgotten Crimean War, Nightingale devoted her life to nursing and social reform; even when poor health immobilized her, she wrote letters to influence public policy and secure funds from philanthropists. Biographer Mark Bostridge reveals that Nightingale was a demanding administrator and influential citizen in this detailed account of her inspiring life.

Bray, Kingsley M.
Crazy Horse: A Lakota Life. 2006. University of Oklahoma Press. 510p. ISBN 0806137851.

The cult of Crazy Horse persists. The Lakota warrior who led more than 200 attacks on his tribe's enemies, including the defeat of George Armstrong Custer at the Little Big Horn, is still revered by Native Americans and their sympathizers. Like his father, Crazy Horse became a tribal elder and fought to protect his people and their lands from the white settlers and soldiers. Using legends of the Lakota Sioux to fill in gaps in Crazy Horse's biography, author Kingsley M. Bray tells a dramatic story about an uncompromising warrior playing his appointed role in history.

Chin, Annping
The Authentic Confucius: A Life of Thought and Politics. 2007. Scribner. 268p. ISBN 9780743246187. 🍃

Most Americans know little about the Chinese philosopher Confucius (551–479 BCE). During his life, few Chinese beyond the region of Lu knew the bureaucrat turned teacher, yet his thoughts became the foundation of Chinese social and political orthodoxy, and he became a larger-than-life figure. Using early historical documents and recent archeological discoveries, Chinese historian Annping Chin strips many fabrications off the Confucius story in this enlightening biography.

Gold, Arthur, and Robert Fizdale
The Divine Sarah: A Life of Sarah Bernhardt. 1991. Alfred A. Knopf. 349p. ISBN 0394528794.

Before Sarah Bernhardt (1844–1923) stepped onto a stage, she was the tempestuous daughter of a Parisian courtesan. After attending a series of private schools, she was given the opportunity to act with the Comédie Française, a struggling theater company in need of rejuvenation. Recognition of her talent came slowly at first, but Bernhardt eventually won praise for her characterizations across Europe and America from luminaries as diverse as Victor Hugo, Mark Twain, and Sigmund Freud. In this admiring biography, authors Arthur Gold and Robert Fizdale recount the fabulous career and stormy relationships of the most celebrated actress of her age.

Gordon, Robert
Can't Be Satisfied: The Life and Times of Muddy Waters. 2002. Little, Brown and Company. 408p. ISBN 0316328499. ♒

Muddy Waters (1913–1983) was born in Rolling Fork, Mississippi, a place so remote that there is no record of his mother's birth, death, or her ever being counted in a census. When folk music historian Alan Lomax discovered the blues musician in 1942, Waters was a sharecropper picking cotton and distilling moonshine. Encouraged by Lomax, Waters headed to Chicago where he began playing in smoky bars and cheap hotels. In this admiring biography, music journalist Robert Gordon recounts the long career of a legendary guitar man who influenced many rock stars, including Bonnie Raitt and the Rolling Stones.

Hazleton, Lesley
Mary: A Flesh-and-Blood Biography of the Virgin Mother. 2004. Bloomsbury. 246p. ISBN 1582342369. ♒

Feeling that the image of Mary, the Mother of Jesus (first century), has been homogenized over time, psychologist Lesley Hazleton has revisited her story. Taking the Gospels and histories of the period, she combines them with psychological insight to create a plausible narrative for the woman she calls Maryam. Readers who value spiritual mediation or enjoy psychological speculation will appreciate this sympathetic biography.

Lovell, Mary S.
The Sound of Wings: The Life of Amelia Earhart. 1989. St. Martin's Press. 420p. ISBN 0312034318.

The disappearance of pilot Amelia Earhart (1897–1937) on her flight around the world is one of the great mysteries of the 20th century. Biographer Mary S. Lovell believes that this tragedy often overshadows the inspiring story of a woman who flew experimental aircraft. In this admiring biography that discounts rumors that Earhart's publicist husband pushed her too hard, Lovell chronicles the life and career of a determined woman whose record-breaking flights made her an international celebrity.

Tye, Larry
Satchel: The Life and Times of an American Legend. 2009. Random House. 392p. ISBN 9781400066513.

Did star Negro League pitcher Satchel Paige (1906–1982) really wave his outfielders off the field and then strike out three opposing batters with the bases loaded? Did he follow his often-repeated rules of never running and avoiding fatty foods to stay young? Incredible stories about the flamboyant athlete are numerous and contradictory. Larry Tye examines Paige's likeable character without overlooking his many faults in this entertaining sports biography.

Exposés

It is shocking but true. Some public figures have lied to us, hiding their crimes and indiscretions. Having protected their reputations in life, they are defenseless in death as confidential records are opened, diary and letters are found, and survivors talk. Among those ready to investigate and publish are biographers. The following exposés featuring politicians, military leaders, industrialist, and celebrities will surprise some unsuspecting readers and confirm the suspicions of others.

Anthony, Carl Sferrazza
Florence Harding: The First Lady, the Jazz Age, and the Death of America's Most Scandalous President. 1998. William Morrow. 645p. ISBN 0688077943. ⬚

First ladies are often thought to be descendants of first-class families and role models of good citizenship. Many thought as much of Florence Harding (1860–1924), wife of the 29th American president. In this somewhat speculative biography, Carl Sferrazza Anthony reveals that Harding was an abused child who became an unwed teenaged mother and later an associate of film stars and gangsters whom she entertained in the White House. Did she also poison the president? Anthony presents evidence in the case.

Bane, Vickie L., and Lorenzo Benet
The Lives of Danielle Steel: The Unauthorized Biography of America's #1 Best-Selling Author. 1994. St. Martin's Press. 307p. ISBN 0312112572.

Novelist Danielle Steel (1947–) would not deny that she has suffered heartbreak, as she has spoken or written about her parents' neglect, her first divorce, and the death of a son. Her upbeat portrayal of her life, however, focuses on success as a writer, wife, and mother. According to journalists Vickie L. Bane and Lorenzo Benet, Steel has deleted many key periods from her official story, including her marriages to criminals and numerous affairs. In this account based on interviews with her colleagues, Bane and Benet describe Steel's life as being as troubled as any of her novels' heroines.

Bergreen, Laurence
Louis Armstrong: An Extravagant Life. 1997. Broadway Books. 564p. ISBN 0553067680.

The lasting image of trumpeter Louis Armstrong (1900–1971) is of an aging performer, nicely dressed and grinning, singing a popular song. According to biographer Laurence Bergreen, the public face of this influential jazz musician hid his temper and subversive tendencies. He was the associate of petty criminals, prostitutes, and other outcasts, and he smoked marijuana as regularly as he took his laxatives. With little sympathy, the author recounts how the deceitful Armstrong fooled the public.

Higham, Charles
Howard Hughes: The Secret Life. 1993. G.P. Putnam's Sons. 368p. ISBN 0399138595.

Thanks to his success supplying equipment for oil fields and building innovative aircraft, Howard Hughes (1905–1976) became one of the 20th century's richest men. Because he was often seen with attractive young actresses, he was the frequent subject of newspaper gossip columns. As his celebrity grew, he became more reclusive, adopting increasingly strange behaviors. In this classic exposé, celebrity biographer Charles Higham recounts the psychological unmaking of a rich and powerful man.

Kelley, Kitty
▶ *His Way: The Unauthorized Biography of Frank Sinatra*. 1986. Bantam Books. 575p. ISBN 0553051377.

Kitty Kelley had already written sensational biographies of Jacqueline Kennedy Onassis and Elizabeth Taylor when she turned her attention to entertainer Frank Sinatra (1915–1998). She acquired FBI documents revealing Sinatra's Mafia connections and interviewed many of his friends and enemies about his violent moods, love affairs, and unhappy childhood. Sinatra sued to stop publication of this book, but Kelley prevailed. This book, which retains its sting, will still interest celebrity readers.

Linklater, Andro
An Artist in Treason: The Extraordinary Double Life of General James Wilkinson. 2009. Walker. 392p. ISBN 9780802717207.

Throughout his long career as a general, first in the Continental Army and then in the army of the new republic, James Wilkinson (1757–1825) was repeatedly suspected of treason, but four congressional investigations failed to find evidence that the popular commander sold secrets to foreign governments. Presidents Washington, Adams, Jefferson, and Madison considered dismissing him, but they feared the troops might side with Wilkinson. Using new sources from the Spanish archives in Madrid, historian Andro Linklater reveals that Wilkinson was Spanish "Agent 13" and linked to the Burr Conspiracy of 1805–1806.

Stiles, T.J.
Jesse James: Last Rebel of the Civil War. 2002. Knopf. 510p. ISBN 0375405836.
☸

An exposé of a famous outlaw might not seem necessary, but Jesse James (1847–1882) has acquired the status of folk hero. Historian T.J. Stiles objects to the softening of James's reputation by apologists who claim that James was just a fighter for Southern causes. In this intense biography, the author strives to prove that James went far beyond crime, enjoying his life as a bushwhacker, white supremacist, and cold-blooded murderer.

Thomas, Anthony
 Rhodes. 1996. St. Martin's Press. 367p. ISBN 0312169825.

In his day, British statesman and financier Cecil Rhodes (1853–1902) was a respected and admired man. Throughout the British Empire, he was famous for extending its territorial claims and for establishing a near monopoly on the production of African diamonds. That Rhodes believed that the British had a sacred duty to subject native populations of the empire to a system of despotism was not considered immoral. Queen Victoria was reportedly grateful for his contributions to the realm. In this passionate exposé, once-exiled South African author Anthony Thomas reveals how a young idealist was turned by power and greed into a racist tyrant who helped prepare South Africa to accept apartheid.

Rebuttals

While some biographers discredit their subjects through detailed exposés, others champion figures that they feel have been misrepresented or misunderstood. An incensed author may challenge a portrayal by another biographer or object to widespread historical opinions about the figure that he or she believes to have been wronged. The advocating biographer retells events and offers new evidence to persuade readers that the subject acted from better motives than previously offered. Here are nine biographies written to defend maligned figures.

Gropman, Donald
 Say It Ain't So, Joe! The Story of Shoeless Joe Jackson. 1979. Little, Brown and Company. 232p. ISBN 0316329258.

Although Joe Jackson was one of Major League Baseball's greatest players, his name is not enrolled in the Hall of Fame in Cooperstown because of his involvement in the 1919 Black Sox Scandal. Banned from professional baseball in 1921, he played for years under false names in obscure minor leagues, hoping for reinstatement. In this quick-paced retelling of the outfield's life, Donald Gropman argued that Shoeless Joe was unfairly punished and deserves reconsideration.

Mackay, James
 Allan Pinkerton: The First Private Eye. 1996. John Wiley & Sons. 256p. ISBN 0471194158.

The private investigator Allan Pinkerton (1819–1884) is often cast as a villain in romanticized portrayals of bank robbers Jesse James, Butch Cassidy, and John Reno, and in books about the Molly Maguires coal miners' strikes. Novels and movies often make him a ruthless servant of the railroads, mine owners, and other rich clients. He is also blamed for bad intelligence that persuaded General McClellan to disobey President Lincoln's order to attack the Confederates in the Civil War. Historian James Mackay objects. The author defends the founder of the Pinkerton Detective Agency in this historical biography.

Norrell, Robert J.

Up from History: The Life of Booker T. Washington. 2009. Belknap Press. 508p. ISBN 9780674032118.

From the perspective of the post–Civil Rights Era, African American educator Booker T. Washington (1856–1915) is often considered with suspicion. Was his advocacy of black rights too timid and passive? Was his vision of the future for his race in America too limited? In this sympathetic full-length biography, historian Robert J. Norrell turns to Jim Crow era documents to discover Washington was a cautious but determined man confident in progress through self-reliance and separation of the races.

Prose, Francine

▶ *Anne Frank: The Book, the Life, the Afterlife*. 2009. Harper. 322p. ISBN 9780061430794.

How readers see Anne Frank (1929–1945), the Jewish girl who hid from the Nazis in war-torn Amsterdam during World War II, has changed for the worse with each release of her famous diary revealing unkind and selfish behavior. Since she was a girl, novelist Francine Prose has followed Frank's reputation, reading each book, interviewing scholars, and visiting Amsterdam. Disagreeing with critics, she profiles Frank's character as stronger than ever in this in-depth account of a life, a book, a play, and a movie.

Rosen, James

The Strong Man: John Mitchell and the Secrets of Watergate. 2008. Doubleday. 609p. ISBN 9780385508643.

Attorney General John Mitchell (1913–1988) was the highest-ranking U.S. government official to ever be imprisoned. A prominent player in the Nixon White House, the former Wall Street lawyer was blamed for rough treatment of antiwar demonstrators, ordering the burglary at the Democratic National Committee headquarters, and involving the CIA in the Watergate cover-up. Unlike most of his White House colleagues, Mitchell never wrote about his role in the scandal and, after completing his prison sentence, was feted by Nixon for being his most loyal friend. Fox News correspondent James Rosen questions the fairness of verdicts and the low public opinion of a man who he believes was a heroic presidential advisor.

Saint Bris, Gonzague

Lafayette: Hero of the American Revolution. 2010. Pegasus Books. 354p. ISBN 9781605980874.

French statesman Gilbert Marie Joseph Paul Yves Roch de Lafayette (1757–1834) is remembered favorably for the aid and encouragement that he brought to the American Revolution. His actions in France, however, are held to have contributed to the disastrously bloody French Revolution. He was exiled from his country, but returned to cautiously serve both the monarchy and the democracy in turn. In this reexamination of Lafayette's long career, French historian Gonzague Saint Bris explains why the Frenchman who compromised his ideals is still worthy of high regard.

Scanlon, Jennifer
  Bad Girls Go Everywhere: The Life of Helen Gurley Brown. 2009. Oxford University Press. 270p. ISBN 9780195342055.

    When *Ms* editor Gloria Steinem charged that *Cosmopolitan* editor Helen Gurley Brown (1922–) was hurting the feminist cause by teaching women to primp for men, Brown argued that through her magazine and her book *Sex and the Single Girl* many women had been sexually liberated and became free to do whatever they pleased. Being a feminist should be fun according to Brown, a married woman criticized as immoral by both right-and left-wing commentators. Gender studies scholar Jennifer Scanlon examines Brown's role in the feminist movement in this approving biography.

Shipman, Pat
  Femme Fatale: Love, Lies, and the Unknown Life of Mata Hari. 2007. William Morrow. 450p. ISBN 9780060817282.

    Indulged by her father as a girl, Margaretha Geertruida Zelle (1876–1918) was distraught at his bankruptcy when she was 13. After living with relatives and failing to become a kindergarten teacher, she married a Scottish army officer who took her to the Dutch West Indies where she failed as a wife and mother. Having observed Oriental dance, the divorcee returned to Europe where under a variety of names she became an exotic dancer, fashionable mistress, and possibly a spy. Using new evidence, author Pat Shipman sympathetically reexamines the life and crimes of an amorous woman remembered as Mata Hari.

Sullivan, Robert
  The Thoreau You Don't Know: What the Prophet of Environmentalism Really Meant. 2009. Collins. 354p. ISBN 9780061710315. ☙

    Living in a cabin on Walden Pond was just one episode in the life of Henry David Thoreau (1817–1862). Detractors point out that he lived most of his life with his parents in the very comfortable town of Concord, Massachusetts, helping with the family business. According to environmental author Robert Sullivan, Thoreau was a struggling author and a gregarious transcendentalist, a serious reformer who could also play humorous pranks on his many friends. Sullivan recounts Thoreau's life and the evolution of his reputation in this updating biography.

Finding Forgotten Heroes

When biographers research their intended subjects, they sometimes discover other figures about whom they know little or nothing. They may change course and write about their newfound subjects or note their discoveries and return years later to write books that they feel must be written. The following books are stories intended to restore the fame and inspire appreciation of once-prominent people who have either been forgotten by readers or overshadowed by their contemporaries.

Boyd, Valerie
Wrapped in Rainbows: The Life of Zora Neale Hurston. 2003. Scribner. 527p. ISBN 0684842300. ☒

When penniless novelist and anthropologist Zora Neale Hurston (1891–1960) was buried in an unmarked grave, all her books were out of print. Her travels across the segregated South, her research in Honduras and Haiti, and her literary years in Harlem were as forgotten as her novels, plays, autobiography, and collections of folklore. In this sympathetic and detailed biography, literary critic Valerie Boyd recounts the life of a passionate and sometimes desperate woman whose *Their Eyes Were Watching God* is now considered a classic of American literature.

Denton, Sally
The Pink Lady: The Many Lives of Helen Gahagan Douglas. 2009. Bloomsbury. 240p. ISBN 9781596914803.

Who left acting for politics long before Ronald Reagan? Who was the victim of one of Richard Nixon's earliest and meanest dirty tricks? Who was the congresswoman who had an affair with Lyndon Johnson? The answer to all three of these questions is Helen Gahagan Douglas (1900–1980). In this admiring biography, journalist Sally Denton recalls the life of a mostly forgotten New Deal politician who sponsored relief for Dust Bowl refugees, affordable housing, public education, and social security, and who spent her later years working for international humanitarian causes.

Dingus, Lowell, and Mark A. Norell
Barnum Brown: The Man Who Discovered Tyrannosaurus Rex. 2010. University of California Press. 368p. ISBN 9780520252646.

In the days of movie newsreels and radio celebrities, paleontologist Barnum Brown (1873–1963) was one of the world's most famous scientists. Fans flocked to remote dig sites just to have their pictures taken with the man who discovered an early Tyrannosaurus Rex. Promising more great finds, Brown charmed sponsors who sent him to desolate regions around the globe. In this admiring biography, authors Lowell Dingus and Mark A. Norell reveal that the charismatic Brown was also an agent for American oil companies and a spy for the U.S. government.

Downey, Kirstin
Woman behind the New Deal: The Life of Frances Perkins, FDR's Secretary of Labor and His Moral Conscience. 2009. Nan A. Talese. 458p. ISBN 9780385513654. ☙

Inspired to a life of service by her Mt. Holyoke College professors and Hull House founder Jane Addams, Frances Perkins (1880–1965) joined the Committee on Safety to study the Triangle Shirtwaist fire in 1911. Twenty-two years later, Franklin D. Roosevelt appointed the tireless champion of working people as secretary of labor. Impressed by the many precedents set by the first woman appointed to the Cabinet, journalist Kirstin Downey spent eight years writing this biography to revive the appreciation of Perkins as one of her century's most accomplished women.

Gray, Michael
Hand Me My Travelin' Shoes: In Search of Blind Willie McTell. 2009. Chicago Review Press. 432p. ISBN 9781556529757.

    Guitarist and singer Blind Willie McTell (1903?–1959) was the first Atlanta-based blues musician signed by Victor Record in 1927. After hearing McTell's records, musicologist John Lomax spent many hours recording the singer's crisp voice and 12-string guitar for the Library of Congress folk music collection. Neither contract brought the bluesman wealth; before he died, he sang for tips from teens parked in cars with their dates. In this investigative biography, British travel writer Michael Gray recounts his search for and discovery of stories about a forgotten musician whose records influenced Bob Dylan.

Hoose, Phillip
Claudette Colvin: Twice toward Justice. 2009. Farrar Strauss Giroux. 133p. ISBN 9780374313227.

    In early 1955, nine months before Rosa Parks also refused to relinquish her seat, teenager Claudette Colvin was arrested for not moving to the back of a Montgomery, Alabama, city bus. Few people praised Colvin for her stand at the time, but she joined the NAACP in a long shot legal case that was eventually won in the U.S. Supreme Court. In this illustrated biography aimed at teens but appropriate for readers of any age, author Phillip Hoose shows how the experience of the forgotten Colvin helped prepare Parks and others to rally for civil rights.

Stoll, Ira
Samuel Adams: A Life. 2008. Free Press. 338p. ISBN 9780743299114.

    No man is more responsible for igniting the American Revolution than Boston's Samuel Adams (1722–1803), who was the earliest and most consistent proponent of colonial liberty. The capture of Adams and John Hancock was a primary object of the British Army's march to Concord and Lexington, and King George himself declared that any scheme to pardon rebels should exclude Adams. Why then is Adams overshadowed by other American patriots? In this biography of Adams's thoughts and actions, journalist Ira Stoll explains how the faithful rebel's selfless sacrifice advanced the American cause at the expense of his own fame and fortune.

Stout, Glenn
▶ *Young Woman and the Sea: How Trudy Ederle Conquered the English Channel and Inspired the World*. 2009. Houghton Mifflin Harcourt. 336p. ISBN 9780618858682.

    As a teenager, Trudy Ederle (1906–2003) won countless national swimming titles and was a key member of the U.S. Olympics team in 1924. She then began training to become the first woman to swim the English Channel, an effort closely followed by American newspapers. Succeeding on her second try, she was honored with a ticker tape parade in New York. Sports historian Glenn Stout profiles the life a young athlete once proclaimed "The World's Most Famous Woman" but then quickly forgotten in the media frenzy of the Roaring Twenties.

Trouble at Home

Ideally, one's home is a refuge from the troubles of daily life, and one's family is compassionate and supportive. In too many cases, however, home becomes a battlefield where spouses and children fight among themselves. In extreme cases, such as the volatile relationship between actors Richard Burton and Elizabeth Taylor or the jealous rivalries among the novel-writing Brontë sisters, the world notices. The following family biographies are some of history's most famous trouble-at-home stories.

Barker, Juliet
The Brontës. 1994. St. Martin's Press. 1003p. ISBN 0312134452.

As curator and librarian for the Brontë Parsonage Museum for six years, Juliet Barker discovered that biographers had relied too much on only a few sources and misjudged relationships between the patriarch Patrick Brontë and his children Charlotte, Emily, Anne, and Bramwell. Their lives were not as bleak as sometimes depicted. Though she dismisses some sensational rumors about the Brontës, Barker still found intense struggles within the talented and closely knit family, whom she portrays together in this large yet intimate biography.

Coll, Steve
Bin Ladens: An Arabian Family in the American Century. 2008. Penguin Press. 671p. ISBN 9781594201646. ♀

Mohamed Bin Laden (1905?–1967) was only a poor bricklayer when he left Yemen to work in Saudi Arabia. Through diligence and astute politics, he became a confidant and business partner of the Saudi royal family, leading to great wealth for him and his 54 children. Pulitzer Prize–winning journalist Steve Coll describes how the secretive Bin Laden family embraced the Western riches and lifestyle that were later rejected by their brother Osama. Coll explains the complicated family response to the September 11, 2001, attacks in this epic family biography.

Gordon-Reed, Annette
The Hemingses of Monticello: An American Family. 2008. W. W. Norton. 798p. ISBN 9780393064773. ♀

From the death of his father-in-law John Wayles in 1773 until his own death in 1826, Thomas Jefferson owned a fair-skinned slave family known as the Hemingses. The mother of the clan was a half-sister of his wife, and two of her children spent years with him during his assignment as ambassador to

France. In her thorough study of the Virginia plantation life, Annette Gordon-Reed recounts more than 40 years of unusual master–slave relations that Jefferson unsuccessfully tried to keep private.

Kashner, Sam, and Nancy Schoenberger
Furious Love: Elizabeth Taylor, Richard Burton, and the Marriage of the Century. 2010. Harper. 500p. ISBN 9780061562846.

When Elizabeth Taylor (1932–2011) first met Richard Burton (1925–1984) nine years before the filming of *Cleopatra*, she disliked his constant inebriated patter. The intimacy of their work on the film set, however, wore away her prejudice and sparked a passionate, hard-fought 13-year affair that ended with their second divorce in 1976. In this retelling of the most reported marriage of its time, *Vanity Fair* editor Sam Kashner and biographer Nancy Schoenberger portray the famous lovers as victims of their inability to separate their public and private lives.

Middlebrook, Diane
▶ *Her Husband: Hughes and Plath—A Marriage*. 2003. Viking. 361p. ISBN 0670031879. ⧢

Four months after meeting at a wild party celebrating the launch of a small literary magazine, Ted Hughes and Sylvia Plath were married. For six years they wrote and read each others' work, faithfully critiquing but always encouraging each other. Then Hughes found another lover, and Plath committed suicide. Biographer and poet Diane Middlebrook revisits the often retold story to focus on Hughes as a spouse before and beyond Plath's death.

Moore, Wendy
Wedlock: The True Story of the Disastrous Marriage and Remarkable Divorce of Mary Eleanor Bowes, Countess of Strathmore. 2009. Crown Publishers. 386p. ISBN 970307383365.

Throughout history, wealthy widows have been the prey of unscrupulous men, who often happened to be charming and handsome. Mary Eleanor Bowes, countess of Strathmore (1749–1800), who was an ancestor of Queen Elizabeth II, was no exception. After being tricked into marrying a rogue who led her to believe he was a dying man, the countess fought back by suing for divorce, a scandalous action for a woman of her time. In this admiring biography, British journalist Wendy Moore recounts the unusual story that inspired William Makepeace Thackeray to write his novel *The Luck of Barry Lyndon*.

Popoff, Alexandra
Sophia Tolstoy: A Biography. 2010. Free Press. 354p. ISBN 9781416597599.

As the mother of his 13 children, the wife who kept his house, and his closest advisor, Sophia Tolstoy (1844–1919) said that her life belonged to her husband, the renowned Russian author Leo Tolstoy. Her loyalty, however, was repaid with his renouncing marriage and sexual relations as evil, and he began depicting all wives as cruel in the books that she still edited and published for him. Her husband's sycophants gossiped that Sophia deserved the rebuke. Using Sophia's recently uncovered writings, Russian journalist Alexandra Popoff reexamines the life of a misrepresented woman who chose not to defend her reputation at the expense of her husband.

Starkey, David

Six Wives: The Queens of Henry VIII. 2003. HarperCollins. 852p. ISBN 069401043X.

What the king wanted was a male heir, but five out of his six queens failed to meet his demand. The one who did died soon after her success. Two were divorced. Two others were beheaded. The story of Henry VIII of England (1491–1547) and his six queens is history's ultimate soap opera, featuring elements of romance, intrigue, horror, and tragedy. Historian David Starkey used many primary sources in this mostly sympathetic collective biography of six unfortunate queens.

Great Rivalries

Fame, wealth, and power are rarely obtained easily. Because there is always someone else who wants these prizes, ambitious people in nearly any field make enemies whom they sometimes fight for the rest of their lives. Golfer Arnold Palmer had to contend with Jack Nicklaus on the leader board, while cosmetics maker Helena Rubinstein always had Eve Arden to best. Astute authors recognize the dramatic appeal a great rivalry adds to their biographical accounts. The following dual biographies feature adversaries in business, science, government, sports, and war.

Clay, Catrine

King, Kaiser, Tsar: Three Royal Cousins Who Led the World to War. 2007. Walker & Company. 416p. ISBN 9780802716231. ☙

Before World War I, three royal cousins reigned over half of the world. By the time they gathered in Berlin for the wedding of German Princess Victoria Louise in 1913, George V of England (1865–1936), Wilhelm II of Germany (1859–1941), and Nicholas II of Russia (1868–1918) had been bickering at family gatherings for four decades. In this psychological biography of the three monarchs, British filmmaker Catrine Clay shows how unchecked family conflict resulted in world war and the deaths of millions.

Hersh, Burton

Bobby and J. Edgar: The Historic Face-Off between the Kennedys and J. Edgar Hoover That Transformed America. 2007. Carroll & Graf. 612p. ISBN 9780786719822.

The enmity between Attorney General Robert Kennedy (1925–1968) and longtime FBI Director J. Edgar Hoover (1895–1972) was based on more than just a disagreement over the direction of 1960s law enforcement. Hoover had quarreled with his rival's father, Joseph P. Kennedy, financier and former U.S. ambassador to Great Britain, over FBI oversight of Kennedy's business interests. Historian Burton Hersh recounts the lives of two men whose intense clashes influenced the fight against organized crime in America.

Levenson, Thomas

Newton and the Counterfeiter: The Unknown Detective Career of the World's Greatest Scientist. 2009. Houghton Mifflin Harcourt. 318p. ISBN 9780151012787.

Many readers know that Sir Isaac Newton (1646–1723) described gravity and light and is heralded as the first real scientist for his adherence to the scientific method. Few know that as warden of the Royal Mint, responsible for the integrity of the king's money, Newton became a pioneering detective who developed criminal investigation procedures. Newton spent years tracking illegally minted coins. Thomas Levenson recounts how the scientist finally caught and convicted his elusive nemesis, the talented counterfeiter William Chaloner (?–1699).

Miller, Arthur I.

Empire of the Stars: Obsession, Friendship, and Betrayal in the Quest for Black Holes. 2005. Houghton Mifflin. 364p. ISBN 061834151X.

Physicists Sir Arthur Eddington (1882–1944) and Subrahmanyan Chandrasekhar (1910–1995) began as friendly colleagues, but then publicly sparred in the halls of the Royal Academy over the existence of black holes created by collapsing stars. The older Englishman demanded that the young man from India give up his theories and bow to the eminence of British science. Arthur I. Miller shares an important story about how scientific progress was subverted by an Englishman's desire to prevail over a colonial subject.

O'Connor, Ian

Arnie and Jack: Palmer, Nicklaus, and Golf's Greatest Rivalry. 2008. Houghton Mifflin. 354p. ISBN 9780618754465.

Arnold Palmer (1929–) was already a pro on the afternoon in 1958 that he first played a round of golf with amateur Jack Nicklaus (1940–). While Palmer won, Nicklaus impressed the golfers at the Athens Country Club that day. For the next 40 years, Nicklaus would win more titles while Palmer won more fans. In this dual biography, sports columnist Ian O'Connor recounts a rivalry that helped define an era of golf.

Ottaviani, Jim, and Big Time Attic

Bone Sharps, Cowboys, and Thunder Lizards: A Tale of Edward Drinker Cope, Othniel Charles Marsh, and the Gilded Age of Paleontology. 2005. G. T. Labs. 165p. ISBN 0966010663.

Despite persistent ridicule from the press and other scientists who did not believe dinosaurs ever existed, a handful of early paleontologists feuded publicly over fossil site claims, naming rights, museum space, and how to reconstruct skeletons. The fight between Edward Drinker Cope (1840–1897) and Othniel Charles Marsh (1813–1899) was so bitter that they hired thugs to vandalize rival digs. Marsh drove Cope into abject poverty, and both died forlorn. In this graphic novel that takes readers into the halls of scientific societies and out to the lawless lands of the western states, Jim Ottaviani retells the story of a tragic rivalry between two fanatical bone diggers in 19th-century America.

Stanton, Tom
Ty and the Babe: Baseball's Fiercest Rivals: A Surprising Friendship and the 1941 Has-Beens Golf Championship. 2007. Thomas Dunne Books. 290p. ISBN 9780312361594.

Detroit Tiger hitting star Ty Cobb (1886–1961) had nothing good to say about the abilities of New York Yankee slugger Babe Ruth (1895–1948). The usually affable Ruth chose not to be baited by Cobb but replied the latter's criticisms by hitting many home runs. Cobb's jealousy and behavior toward Ruth worsened through his career on the ball field. Unexpectedly, retirement softened the rivalry and the Baseball Hall-of-Famers eventually became golfing buddies. Sportswriter Tom Stanton recounts the change in the hearts of opponents in this entertaining dual biography.

Weintraub, Stanley
15 Stars: Eisenhower, MacArthur, Marshall: Three Generals Who Saved the American Century. 2007. Free Press. 541p. ISBN 9780743275279. ☙

By Act of Congress in December, 1944, Dwight Eisenhower (1890–1969), Douglas MacArthur (1880–1964), and George C. Marshall (1880–1959) became five-star generals, leveling their ranks of authority. The three celebrated career soldiers, who had spent decades leapfrogging each other in the U.S. military chain of command, were challenged to work together to win World War II. In this detailed group portrait, author Stanley Weintraub examines their sometimes difficult relationships and explains why Eisenhower was the one to become president.

Woodhead, Lindy
▶ *War Paint: Madame Helena Rubinstein and Miss Elizabeth Arden, Their Lives, Their Times, Their Rivalry*. 2003. John Wiley & Sons. 492p. ISBN 0471487783.

Opposites attract, likes repel. Cosmetics pioneers Helena Rubinstein of Poland (1870–1965) and Elizabeth Arden of Canada (1878–1966) were very alike, strong-willed women who rose from poverty to establish multimillion dollar companies that propelled them into high society of New York, London, and Paris. Both saw the potential of selling cosmetics and perfumes just as women began to have disposable income. Though they never met, they fought ruthlessly to outdo each other through magazines ads and promotions at the cosmetics counters. Fashion journalist Lindy Woodhead recounts the lives of two remarkable women in this admiring dual biography.

Fragile Friendships

"No man is an island," wrote poet John Donne. People are meant to live and work together, and bonding in friendship is one of life's joys. Forming and maintaining friendships, however, is not always easy. People from different backgrounds, such as tennis players Althea Gibson and Angela Buxton, take time finding each other. Gender issues may strain good friendships, such as that between abolitionist Frederick Douglass and journalist Ottilie Assing. Colleagues, such as philosophers Hannah Arendt and Martin Heidegger, can be separated by war. The following titles examine the lives of remarkable individuals touched by friendship.

Ambrose, Stephen E.
Comrades: Brothers, Fathers, Heroes, Sons, Pals. 1999. Simon & Schuster. 139p. ISBN 0684867184.

In other books, historian Stephen E. Ambrose wrote at greater length about most of the subjects collected in this short volume about bonding among famous companions, including the soldiers in his book *Band of Brothers* and the explorers Meriwether Lewis and William Clark in *Undaunted Courage*. The strength of these profiles lies in the warm intimacy with which Ambrose wrote. This quick-reading book serves as an introduction to Ambrose's writing and a tribute to men who realize they need friends.

Cheever, Susan
American Bloomsbury: Louisa May Alcott, Ralph Waldo Emerson, Margaret Fuller, Nathaniel Hawthorne, and Henry David Thoreau: Their Lives, Their Loves, Their Work. 2006. Simon & Schuster. 223p. ISBN 9780743264617.

In the 1840s and 1850s, Concord, Massachusetts, was the home of a remarkable group of novelists and essayists, collectively known as the Transcendentalists, who influenced the course of American literature. With Ralph Waldo Emerson as the central figure, they discussed philosophy and the issues of the day while helping each other with their writings and daily lives. Author Susan Cheever skillfully profiles the individuals and their relationships in this entertaining quick read.

Diedrich, Maria
Love across Color Lines: Ottilie Assing and Frederick Douglass. 1999. Hill and Wang. 480p. ISBN 0809016133. ⧠

For 28 years, African American abolitionist Frederick Douglass (1818–1895) and German journalist Ottilie Assing (1819–1884) worked together for social reform, openly seeking each others' company and writing letters when apart, challenging the conventions of race, class, and gender. With Douglass married, their relationship never became visibly romantic, but in her diaries, Assing admitted her hopes for future love. In this dual biography, historian

Maria Diedrich recounts the story of an ultimately thwarted relationship in times of abolition, war, and reconstruction.

Hadju, David

Positively 4th Street: The Lives and Times of Joan Baez, Bob Dylan, Mimi Baez Fariña and Richard Fariña. 2001. Farrar, Straus and Giroux. 328p. ISBN 0374281998.

In the late 1950s and the early 1960s, the coffeehouses of Greenwich Village in New York attracted young folk musicians from across the country. Among the rising stars were sisters Joan and Mimi Baez, who soon encountered new friends Richard Fariña and Bob Dylan. According to author David Hadju, their short and sometimes volatile time as friends and lovers developed their talents and set a course for the development of folk rock music. Hadju recounts the quartet's collaborations and betrayals in this critical group biography.

Halberstam, David

▶ *The Teammates: A Portrait of Friendship*. 2003. Hyperion. 217p. ISBN 140130057X.

A quartet of baseball players from the 1940s era Boston Red Sox remained close friends for 60 years. The most famous of the four was the great hitter Ted Williams, an emotional man whose aloofness alienated some fans and tested the patience of his best friends—Dom DiMaggio, Johnny Pesky, and Bobby Doerr. For this heartwarming book, best-selling author David Halberstam drew on interviews with the men to show how good teammates can become friends forever.

Lingeman, Richard

Double Lives: American Writers' Friendships. 2006. Random House. 255p. ISBN 1400060451.

Writers are said to make terrible friends, especially for other writers. Jealousy often plays a hand in spoiling relationships, and writers are prone to reveal what was said in confidence. Despite these handicaps, biographer Richard Lingeman reports that some writers forged lasting and beneficial friendships. He even argues that Ernest Hemingway and F. Scott Fitzgerald stayed friends until the latter's death in this collection of short biographical pieces.

Maier-Katkin, Daniel

Stranger from Abroad: Hannah Arendt, Martin Heidegger, Friendship, and Forgiveness. 2010. W. W. Norton. 384p. ISBN 9780393068337.

Can friendship survive being wartime enemies? German philosopher Martin Heidegger (1889–1976) embraced the Nazi regime of Adolf Hitler, whereas his Jewish student and former lover Hannah Arendt (1906–1975) fled to America to escape the Holocaust. After the war, the Jewish community criticized Arendt for renewing her friendship with Heidegger, who never apologized for his anti-Semitism. In this intimate dual biography, Daniel Maier-Katkin recounts the history of an unlikely friendship.

Schoenfeld, Bruce

The Match: Althea Gibson and Angela Buxton: How Two Outsiders—One Black, the Other Jewish—Forged a Friendship and Made Sports History. 2004. Amistad. 304p. ISBN 0060526521.

The title summarizes the plot well. African American Althea Gibson (1927–2003) rose from poverty to break the color barrier in tennis, while Jewish player Angela Buxton (1934–) emigrated from South Africa to England where she became the first British woman to make the Wimbledon final in 17 years. Because neither was popular with their contemporaries, they played together, won numerous doubles championships, and became friends. In this dual biography, author Bruce Schoenfeld continues the story beyond their tennis years, showing how their relationship matured.

Wineapple, Brenda

White Heat: The Friendship of Emily Dickinson and Thomas Wentworth Higginson. 2008. Alfred A. Knopf. 416p. ISBN 9781400044016. 🐌

Poet Emily Dickinson (1830–1886) wrote to author and abolitionist Thomas Wentworth Higginson (1823–1911) out of the blue because she sensed that he was a compassionate man with a willing ear, starting a friendship maintained mostly by letters. When Dickinson died, Higginson was enlisted in the effort to publish her poetry in a manner that her sister and the public would accept. In this dual biography, Brenda Wineapple recounts a remarkable friendship formed at a time of Victorian sensibilities when Dickinson's poetry was considered quite shocking.

Chapter Three

Setting

L. Frank Baum, author of *The Wonderful Wizard of Oz*, knew about our human interest in places real or imagined. After visiting the beautiful white city of the World Columbian Exposition in Chicago in 1893, he created a marvelous fictional world that was a deceptively dangerous setting for the adventures of a girl from Kansas and her unusual assortment of friends. Readers cheered and wanted to return to Oz many times, and Baum reluctantly wrote sequels. You can read more about the worlds that Baum inhabited and created in the biography *The Real Wizard of Oz: The Life and Times of L. Frank Baum*, which is included in this chapter on biographical settings.

Like Baum, biographers understand the importance of setting as an anchor for their accounts about famous people. Forces from the environments in which they lived shaped these people, and how they responded to the events of their eras was what made them worthy of fame. Luckily for readers, many biographers take great care in researching and recreating the worlds in which their subjects lived. As a result, you may enjoy reading about Jane Boleyn in the court of Henry VIII, Michelangelo in the world of the Italian Renaissance, John James Audubon on the American frontier, or Beau Brummell in London's high society.

In this chapter are 12 book lists featuring biographies of people in similar settings. The chapter starts with "Off the Map" and "On the Frontier," lists in which the settings are geographical and protagonists are challenged by natural environments. As the chapter progresses, settings transform from physical places to cultural spaces. "On Stage and Screen" and "With Beakers or Binoculars" collect biographies in the intense worlds of entertainment and science. The final lists are "In the Court of the King and Queen" and "In High Society," in which subjects negotiate the hierarchies of caste and politics.

Off the Map

Since the invention of the printing press, readers have prized books by adventurous men and women describing their exploits in previously unexplored places. Although there are now very few isolated places remaining, readers still enjoy stories about the dangers faced by Alexander von Humboldt wandering the jungles of South America and Robert Falcon Scott crossing the Antarctic ice. The following biographies describe brave explorers in exotic lands that were just white spaces on the map in their day.

Crane, David
Scott of the Antarctic: A Life of Courage and Tragedy. 2006. Alfred A. Knopf. 572p. ISBN 0375415270.

Before British explorer Robert Falcon Scott (1868–1912) led an expedition to be the first to reach the South Pole, two things were known about Antarctica between Ross Island and the Pole—the distance and the cold. Not knowing about the topography or the frequency of storms, he generously calculated days needed for the journey and provisions to be stationed along the way. He was neither foolish nor blindly heroic, according to author David Crane. Crane describes Scott as a proven leader and a concerned family man in this adventure biography.

Fischer, David Hackett
Champlain's Dream. 2008. Simon & Schuster. 834p. ISBN 9781416593324.

French sea captain and explorer Samuel de Champlain (1567–1635) is remembered as the "Father of New France." In a 37-year period, he led 27 Atlantic crossings without losing a single ship and explored 6 Canadian provinces and 5 American states on foot. During that time, he was also an important member of the French royal court, military leader, historian, naturalist, and cartographer. In this epic biography with lengthy appendices, historian David Hackett Fischer portrays Champlain as a remarkably diplomatic man of vision who was religiously tolerant and usually peaceful in his relations with Native Americans.

Gould, Carol Grant
The Remarkable Life of William Beebe: Explorer and Naturalist. 2004. Island Press/Shearwater Books. 447p. ISBN 1559638583.

Zoologist William Beebe (1877–1962) was a romantic figure who led nearly 50 expeditions to isolated locations—even the ocean floor—for the New York Zoological Society and the American Museum of Natural History. Due to his position as director of the society's Department of Tropical Studies and the wide popularity of his travel memoirs, he knew every important conscrvationist from Teddy Roosevelt to Rachel Carson. He also knew Noel Coward, Will Rogers, and many smart, beautiful women. Carol Grant Gould recounts his many adventures and relationships in this admiring biography.

Helferich, Gerald

Humboldt's Cosmos: Alexander von Humboldt and the Latin American Journey That Changed the Way We See the World. 2004. Gotham Books. 358p. ISBN 1592400523.

In the early 19th century, Alexander von Humboldt and his companion Aimé Bolpland traversed the jungles of the Amazon and the heights of the Andes in search of unknown plants and natural wonders. They spent five years collecting and recording their findings. With their many specimens, they then toured the United States to great acclaim. Gerald Helferich recounts the life of the naturalist who inspired Thomas Jefferson and a host of American explorers to map their country and the world.

Jeal, Tim

▶ *Stanley: The Impossible Life of Africa's Greatest Explorer*. 2007. Yale University Press. 570p. ISBN 9780300126259. ⏧

While the African adventures of explorer Henry Morton Stanley (1841–1904) were celebrated in his lifetime, he has been portrayed in recent years as a pawn of Belgian King Leopold II. He has been charged with willfully causing tribal unrest and profiting from enslaving rubber plantation workers. Using newly available diaries and letters, historian Tim Jeal defends Stanley, whom he claims regretted the harm he unwittingly brought to the continent that he explored.

MacIntyre, Ben

The Man Who Would Be King: The First American in Afghanistan. 2004. Farrar, Straus & Giroux. 351p. ISBN 0374201781.

American sailor Josiah Harlan (1799–1871) was a desperate young man recently betrayed by his fiancée when he jumped ship in Calcutta and crossed into the unknown lands of Afghanistan, where he discovered an ongoing war between local tribes. Pledging his allegiance to a series of Afghan princes, he gained power and claimed the title of Prince of Ghor. In this adventure biography, historian Ben MacIntyre recounts the life of a mercenary who became the model for Rudyard Kipling's tragic story *The Man Who Would Be King*.

McGoogan, Ken

Ancient Mariner: The Arctic Adventures of Samuel Hearne, the Sailor Who Inspired Coleridge's Masterpiece. 2004. Carroll & Graf Publishers. 333p. ISBN 0786713046.

That British explorer Samuel Hearne (1745–1792) dreamed of being a clergyman before he joined the Royal Navy at 12 was a clue to his character. Unlike many of his contemporaries, he ultimately questioned how the Navy treated common sailors and later how the Hudson Bay Company for whom he worked cheated and deliberately killed the Inuit of northern Canada. Hearne described his Arctic explorations and laments to the poet Samuel Taylor Coleridge, who penned "The Rime of the Ancient Mariner." In this historical biography, author Ken McGoogan recounts the conduct of an uncommon explorer.

Millard, Candice
The River of Doubt: Theodore Roosevelt's Darkest Journey. 2005. Doubleday. 416p. ISBN 0385507968. ☽

> After losing the presidential election to Woodrow Wilson in 1912, Theodore Roosevelt (1858–1919) was without a political office and open for adventure. As originally conceived, his South American journey was to be simply sightseeing, but that changed when his expedition set off for the uncharted River of Doubt. Poisonous snakes, piranha, waterfalls, and high fevers awaited the intrepid former president. Author Candice Millard vividly recounts Roosevelt's arduous descent of the danger-filled river.

On the Frontier

Explorers saw what there was to see in new lands and then returned to the cities to report. The bravest people may have been the Daniel Boones and the Granville Stuarts who followed the explorers to settle beyond the boundaries of safety and established frontier communities. With their families in tow, they risked their fortunes and lives to farm and found new towns. The following biographies tell the stories of hardworking people of the frontier.

Christian, Shirley
Before Lewis and Clark: The Story of the Chouteaus, the French Dynasty That Ruled the American Frontier. 2004. Farrar, Straus & Giroux. 509p. ISBN 0374110050. ☽

> Know the Chouteaus? Despite the family's prominence along the frontier of the Mississippi and Missouri Rivers in the 18th and early 19th centuries, they are absent from most history texts. Jean Pierre Chouteau (1758–1849), son of St. Louis pioneer Pierre de Laclède, extended the family's control of the mid-American fur trade, real estate, and banking—all before the Lewis and Clark expedition began. In this fascinating family biography, historian Shirley Christian depicts early pioneers with surprising vision and political clout.

Jones, Landon Y.
William Clark and the Shaping of the West. 2004. Hill and Wang. 394p. ISBN 9780809030415.

> While he is most famous as an explorer for crossing the North American continent with Meriwether Lewis, William Clark's (1770–1831) role as an important soldier, surveyor, and statesman is often overlooked. As a youth, he

helped settle Kentucky, and after his famous expedition, he spent 30 years negotiating Indian treaties and promoting settlement of the states of the Midwest. He even became governor of Missouri. In this admiring biography, historian Landon Y. Jones portrays Clark as a steady man who overcame personal misfortune to lead the nation west.

Miller, John E.
Becoming Laura Ingalls Wilder: The Woman behind the Legend. 1998. University of Missouri Press. 306p. ISBN 0826211674.

In her beloved *Little House* books, Laura Ingalls Wilder (1867–1957) vividly told the story of a girl growing up in the American Midwest. Readers learned much about daily life in frontier Wisconsin, Minnesota, Oklahoma, and South Dakota. In this admiring biography, historian John E. Miller clarifies Wilder's fictionalized accounts and completes her story by telling about her life with husband Almanzo in rural Missouri, where she eventually wrote her books.

Milner, Clyde A., II, and Carol A. O'Connor
As Big as the West: The Pioneer Life of Granville Stuart. 2009. Oxford University Press. 430p. ISBN 9780195127096.

Few people witnessed as much America's pioneer history as Granville Stuart (1834–1918). He moved to the newly opened Iowa Territory at age four, joined the rush to the California gold fields in 1850, married a Shoshone woman, herded cattle in Montana, led vigilantes who hung suspected outlaws, and kept meticulous records of it all. He even drew sketches of the wildlife and landscape. Using Stuart's two-volume autobiography and extensive papers, historians Clyde A. Milner II and Carol A. O'Connor recount the full life of a pioneer who embodied everything good and bad about American westward expansion.

Morgan, Robert
▶ *Boone: A Biography*. 2007. Algonquin Books of Chapel Hill. 538p. ISBN 9781565124554.

Frontiersman Daniel Boone (1734–1820) never wore a coonskin cap and was not the first white settler in Kentucky. Contrary to legends, he was not illiterate and took up arms against Native Americans reluctantly. Instead, he was a thoughtful and well-spoken community leader looking to make a comfortable home for his family. In this admiring historical biography, poet and novelist Robert Morgan portrays the noted woodsman as an early environmentalist and advocate for wilderness, a man both of and ahead of his time.

Rhodes, Richard
John James Audubon: The Making of an American. 2004. Knopf. 514p. ISBN 0375414126.

Arriving in America in 1803, John James Audubon (1785–1851) witnessed and reported on the opening of the American West through his letters and striking illustrations of the continent's birds. His art and storytelling made him famous in his time and helped to drive the settling of territories, but he fared poorly as a businessman and was often in debt. In this detailed biography, Richard Rhodes recounts the life of a man more at home in the woods than in the society that he hoped would buy his books and paintings.

Taylor, Alan
William Cooper's Town: Power and Persuasion on the Frontier of the Early American Republic. 1995. Alfred A. Knopf. 549p. ISBN 0394580540.

By being a partner in the founding of Cooperstown, New York, in the 1780s, land speculator William Cooper (1754–1809) gained more than wealth. He also acquired economic and political power, which he used to become an Otsego County judge and U.S. Senator. Though credited with making property affordable for settlers, Cooper's control of banking, government, and real estate dispersal eventually bred resentment and opposition. In this political biography, historian Alan Taylor recounts how Cooper lost his influence and became a model for corrupt politicians in novels written by his son, James Fenimore Cooper.

VanderVelde, Lea
Mrs. Dred Scott: A Life on Slavery's Frontier. 2009. Oxford University Press. 480p. ISBN 9780195366563

Who was Mrs. Dred Scott, wife of the slave whose claim for freedom was denied by the U.S. Supreme Court in 1857? According to Lea VanderVelde, Harriet Robinson was a black woman born in Virginia around 1818 and taken to the supposedly free Northwest Territory in 1835, where she met and married Etheldred Scott, a slave at Fort Snelling. To make up for the scarcity of stories about Scott, the author thoroughly describes her work and situation in frontier Minnesota and later in boomtown St. Louis, Missouri.

On the Seven Seas

In mid-ocean, there are only waves, seabirds, and endless sky. How could anyone live and work under such stark conditions? To the wonder of land-bound readers, some hardy people flourish away from shore while crossing the oceans in search of adventure, commerce, science, or solitude. Captain Joshua Slocum even circled the earth quite happily alone. The following biographies recount the drama of remarkable maritime lives.

Colley, Linda
The Ordeal of Elizabeth Marsh: A Woman in World History. 2007. Pantheon Books. 363p. ISBN 9780375421532.

Most 18th-century women stayed home when their men went to sea. As the daughter of an officer in the Royal Navy and later as the wife of a British merchant, Elizabeth Marsh (1735–1785) spent much of her life on ships sailing back and forth from her native England to the distant ports of the British Empire. Recognizing the growing English interest in exotic lands, she wrote numerous travel books that she sold through subscriptions. Having read Marsh's surviving works, author Linda Colley recounts the traveler's life and the world that she described.

Cordingly, David
Cochrane: The Real Master and Commander. 2007. Bloomsbury. 420p. ISBN 9781582345345.

Novelists Patrick O'Brian, C. S. Forester, and Captain Marryat had a common model for their naval heroes: Lord Thomas Cochrane (1775–1860), a celebrated admiral of the Royal Navy. In his battles with the French Navy and his campaigns to liberate Chile, Peru, and Brazil from the Spanish and the Portuguese, he won the hearts of the British public and the friendship of Lord Byron and Sir Walter Scott. With many maps, drawings, and paintings included, David Cordingly, keeper of pictures and head of exhibitions at the National Maritime Museum in Greenwich, vividly recounts the life of a man who looked for glory at sea.

Dugard, Martin
▶ *Farther Than Any Man: The Rise and Fall of Captain James Cook*. 2001. Pocket Books. 287p. ISBN 0743400682. 🐚

The Pacific Ocean was mostly unmapped when Captain James Cook (1728–1779) led the first of his three expeditions. At sea for nearly 12 years, he located many islands, including Australia, New Zealand, and Tahiti, and was the first European to encounter many native peoples. He and his crew were sometimes chased away with spears, but they usually traded goods (and diseases) with the islanders. Refusing entreaties to retire to England to enjoy his fame, Cook was eventually killed by natives in Hawaii. In this sympathetic account, Martin Dugard portrays Cook as a well-meaning explorer who stayed at his job too long.

Preston, Diana, and Michael Preston
A Pirate of Exquisite Mind: Explorer, Naturalist, and Buccaneer: The Life of William Dampier. 2004. Walker & Company. 372p. ISBN 0802714250.

Life at sea has always appealed to complex characters. The hydrologist and naturalist William Dampier (1651–1715) was such a man, a charming buccaneer who charted ocean currents and described exotic birds when not attacking Spanish treasure ships. Stealing from his nation's enemy and writing best-selling books made him seem more patriot than pirate. Diana Preston and Michael Preston recount the adventures of a seafaring man admired by novelists and poets.

Thomas, Evan
John Paul Jones: Sailor, Hero, Father of the American Navy. 2003. Simon & Schuster. 383p. ISBN 0743205839.

After escaping from Scottish farm life as a youth, naval hero John Paul Jones (1747–1792) spent much of his short life at sea, first as an apprentice on a merchant ship, then as second mate on a slave ship, and eventually as captain of the American warship *Bonhomme Richard*. As captain, he developed a reputation for cunning and courage and renown for declaring "I have not yet begun to fight."

Unfortunately for Jones, the end of the American Revolution left him unemployed, leading him to join the Russian Navy. He died in Paris before receiving a new American commission. In this admiring biography, *Newsweek* editor Evan Thomas seeks to restore the reputation of a forgotten revolutionary hero.

Whitfield, Peter

Sir Francis Drake. 2004. New York University Press. 160p. ISBN 081479403.

As a commander in the English fleet during the attack by the Spanish Armada, Sir Francis Drake (1540?–1596) was considered a great British hero both in his time and for centuries afterward. He was already famous for circumnavigating the global and boldly attacking treasure-laden ships of Spain and other British enemies. As a favorite of Queen Elizabeth I, he was welcomed at court and forgiven many acts that other nations considered crimes. In this beautifully illustrated and concise biography, historian Peter Whitfield scrutinizes Drake's questionable reputation.

Wolff, Geoffrey

The Hard Way Around: The Passages of Joshua Slocum. 2010. Alfred A. Knopf. 218p. ISBN 9781400043422.

In 1898, when Captain Joshua Slocum (1844–1908?) completed a solo voyage around the earth in the 37-foot sloop that he built by hand, some newspaper editors refused to believe his claim. He could not have done it alone, they argued. The controversy spurred sales of his book *Sailing Alone around the World*. In this admiring account, novelist Geoffrey Wolff recounts the adventurous life of a headstrong sailor who survived shipwrecks, storms, mutinies, and pirate attacks but ultimately disappeared at sea.

Zacks, Richard

The Pirate Hunter: The True Story of Captain Kidd. 2002. Theia. 426p. ISBN 0786865334.

The good name of Captain William Kidd (1645–1701) has been wronged, according to author Richard Zacks. Kidd was not an evil pirate as portrayed by dime-store novelists but was a pirate hunter backed by colonial merchants seeking to have their stolen goods returned. With his eye on winning bounties, the hard-nosed Kidd sailed into lawless waters to confront cutthroats, including his archrival Robert Culliford. In this revisionist biography, Zacks recreates the historic age of piracy from which many legends come.

Behind the Battle Lines

There is significance in the often-heard statement "the nation is at war." Soldiers are not the only people hurt by the bullets and the bombs. Citizens in the line of fire become collateral damage. Occupied cities, such as Warsaw in World War II, become oppressive. Even oceans away, families are broken apart by conflicts that take their sons, daughters, husbands, and wives. The following biographies recount the lives of noncombatants who struggled for emotional or physical survival in times of war.

Ackerman, Diane

▶ *The Zookeeper's Wife: A War Story*. 2007. W. W. Norton. 367p. ISBN 9780393061727. ☒

When the Nazis invaded Poland in 1939, they set out to exterminate Jews, Catholics, and Gypsies and transform the country into a land filled with Germanic people. Even fair-haired Poles like Antonina Żabiński (1908–?) were endangered if they did not adhere strictly to German rules. As keepers of the Warsaw Zoo, Antonina and her husband Jan were in a unique position to secretly break many dictates of their new overlords. In this admiring biography, essayist and poet Diane Ackerman recounts how the brave couple saved the lives of many Jews, Catholics, and members of the Polish resistance.

Atkinson, Diane

Elsie and Mairi Go to War: Two Extraordinary Women on the Western Front. 2010. Pegasus Books. 280p. ISBN 9781605980942.

Thirty-year-old divorcee Elsie Knocker and 18-year-old tomboy Mairi Chisholm were unlikely friends brought together by their love of motorcycles. When Great Britain declared war against Germany in 1914, they volunteered to drive an ambulance in Belgium. Together they redefined the role by setting up a first-aid post close to the trenches, for which they were awarded medals by the Belgian king and the queen of Great Britain. In this dual biography, women's historian Diane Atkinson tells a story of brave friends whose fame cheered up troops and the British public.

Berkin, Carol

Civil War Wives: The Lives and Times of Angelina Grimké Weld, Varina Howell Davis, and Julia Dent Grant. 2009. Alfred A. Knopf. 361p. ISBN 9781400044467.

During the years leading up to the American Civil War, upper-class women in both northern and southern states achieved unprecedented levels of education and joined in reform movements that sometimes conflicted with their husbands' interests. Setting aside concerns and aspirations proved difficult, even in times of war. Using diaries, letters, and memoirs, feminist scholar Carol Berkin intimately recounts the wartime experiences of three women whose husbands demanded their unwilling subservience and loyalty.

Mortimer, Gavin

Double Death: The True Story of Pryce Lewis, the Civil War's Most Daring Spy. 2010. Walker & Company. 285p. ISBN 9780802717696.

When young flannel weaver Pryce Lewis (1831–1911) left England for America in 1856, he wanted a new occupation and some adventure. He found both when he joined the Pinkerton Detective Agency just before the start of the Civil War. With his knowledge of the textile trade, he posed as an English buyer of cotton to travel through the Confederate States as a Union spy. In this compelling biography, British journalist Gavin Mortimer recounts the dangerous life of a spy whose reports to Union generals and President Lincoln exposed enemy spies and revealed Confederate battle plans.

Oates, Stephen B.
A Woman of Valor: Clara Barton and the Civil War. 1994. Free Press. 526p. ISBN 0029234050.

Clara Barton (1821–1912) was working in the U.S. Patent Office in Washington, D.C. when she heard that soldiers from her native state of Massachusetts were attacked by a mob in Baltimore. She rushed to the train depot to see if she could help care for these first casualties of the Civil War. In the next four years, she nursed thousands of wounded soldiers in makeshift hospitals beside the bloodiest battlefields. In this biography focusing on Barton's first war, historian Stephen B. Oates portrays his subject as a determined woman unwilling to let her own health or loneliness keep her from her mission.

Olson, Lynne
Citizens of London: The Americans Who Stood with Britain in Its Darkest, Finest Hour. 2010. Random House. 471p. ISBN 9781400067589.

In the spring of 1941, when only Great Britain held out against the Axis powers of Hitler and Mussolini, three Americans joined the beleaguered people of London in their war-torn streets. John Gilbert Winant (1889–1947) was the new American ambassador, Edward R. Murrow (1908–1965) was CBS Radio's ace reporter, and Averell Harriman (1891–1986) was America's Land-Lease administrator, responsible for bringing aid to the British. All were welcome in the office and home of Prime Minister Winston Churchill. In this tightly woven joint biography, journalist Lynne Olson admiringly recounts how the trio prepared the way for President Franklin Roosevelt to befriend Churchill and bring their country into the war.

Roberts, Cokie
Founding Mothers: The Women Who Raised Our Nation. 2004. HarperCollins. 359p. ISBN 0060090251. ⬚

Would Americans have won the war for independence from Great Britain without the support of women on the home front? Journalist Cokie Roberts thinks not. In this collective biography of the wives and daughters of the Founding Fathers, Roberts vividly recounts the lives of Martha Washington, Abigail Adams, Mercy Otis Warren, and other women who raised children, farmed, and ran businesses while their men were at war.

Roper, Robert
Now the Drum of War: Walt Whitman and His Brothers in the Civil War. 2008. Walker & Company. 421p. ISBN 9780802715531. ⬚

Though the face of Walt Whitman (1819–1892) is recognized by many modern readers, he was known only to literate East Coast society in his day. By the start of the Civil War, he had published three editions of *Leaves of Grass*, written and edited for several newspapers, met Emerson and Thoreau, and, although he prospered by building houses in Brooklyn, he was still living with his mother and brothers. In this slice-of-life biography, Robert Roper recounts how Whitman became an angel of mercy to his family and many wounded soldiers during a war noted for making brothers enemies.

In the Heat of Battle

The life of the soldier in the context of war has been the subject of literature since *The Iliad* by Homer. Authors of fiction, history, and biography have continually written about the infantry who showed courage and determination in the face of danger and the generals who led the charges into battle. The following biographies represent the stories of fighters that will attract readers wishing either to understand their own times or to imagine wars of the past.

Arthur, Anthony
General Jo Shelby's March. 2010. Random House. 265p. ISBN 9781400068302.

As a cavalry commander throughout the American Civil War, Confederate general Jo Shelby (1830–1897) was renowned for surprise attacks and daring charges that were cheered across the South. Unwilling to lay down his arms after peace was declared at Appomattox, he led 300 men deep into Mexico where he hoped to rekindle the Southern cause and possibly take control of the Mexican government. After a tense year and a half of courting favor from both Emperor Maximilian and rebel Benito Juarez, Shelby narrowly escaped Mexico with his life. In this frank but admiring biography of a man who spent his final days as a U.S. Marshal, author Anthony Arthur portrays Shelby as a soldier who enjoyed the tactics of war.

Kozak, Warren
LeMay: The Life and Wars of General Curtis LeMay. 2009. Regnery. 434p. ISBN 9781596985698.

Air Force Chief Curtis LeMay (1906–1990) was not a man to apologize for anything, including the firebombing of cities. He was known as a fearless leader who even as a general flew the lead aircraft in dangerous World War II missions. In this quick-reading reassessment of a long military career, journalist Warren Kozak portrays LeMay as a pragmatic and often-controversial military strategist who helped shape American military policy through the first half of the Cold War.

Krakauer, Jon
Where Men Win Glory: The Odyssey of Pat Tillman. 2009. Doubleday. 383p. ISBN 9780385522267. ♋

Pat Tillman (1976–2004) was not a career soldier looking for promotion or military honors. Instead, he was a free-spirited, well-paid professional football player who volunteered to help his country fight al-Qaeda and the Taliban in Afghanistan. His well-publicized enlistment and the cover-up of his friendly fire death in battle were news headlines that fed into the contentious debate over the validity of the U.S. military efforts in the Middle East. Using Tillman's diaries and letters as well as interviews with his family and friends, best-selling author Jon Krakauer examines a complicated man and his reasons for becoming a soldier.

Lacey, Jim

Pershing. 2008. Palgrave Macmillan. 206p. ISBN 9780230603837.

Born just before the American Civil War, John J. Pershing (1860–1948) is considered by many scholars to be the architect of the modern U.S. Army. During his career, he fought in the Indian Wars, the Spanish–American War, the Philippines Insurgency, and the 1916 invasion of Mexico in search of Pancho Villa. He is most remembered for his bloody but successful campaign to defeat the German Army during World War I. Defense analyst Jim Lacey describes Pershing as a determined and innovative general in this sympathetic and quickly read biography.

Lengel, Edward G.

▶ *General George Washington: A Military Life*. 2005. Random House. 450p. ISBN 1400060818.

Having witnessed the slaughter of troops in the French and Indian War, George Washington (1732–1799) knew the military consequences of arrogant and incompetent leadership. The odds of his lightly armed Patriot volunteers defeating King George's well-provisioned professional army were poor, and he could not afford to make mistakes. In this admiring biography, historian Edward G. Lengel tells why the less experienced citizen-soldier Washington was able to outlast and outsmart the British generals on the battlefield.

McLynn, Frank

Heroes and Villains: Inside the Minds of the Greatest Warriors in History. 2009. Pegasus Books. 384p. ISBN 9781605980294.

What drives military leaders to risk their own safety and the fortunes of their nations to invade other lands? Can there be any noble reasons behind conquest? Feeling that warriors are often unfairly described as ambitious and brutal, British historian Frank McLynn psychologically profiles six of history's most controversial warlords: Spartacus, Attila the Hun, Richard the Lionhearted, Hernando Cortés, Tokugawa Ieyasu, and Napoleon Bonaparte.

Proser, Jim, with Jerry Cutter

I'm Staying with My Boys: The Heroic Life of Sgt. John Basilone, USMC. 2010. St. Martin's Griffin. 336p. ISBN 9780312611446.

For his leadership, bravery, and sacrifice in battles at both Guadalcanal and Iwo Jima, Sgt. John Basilone (1916–1945) was one of the most decorated marines of World War II. He was also a beloved friend about whom many of his colleagues have stories. Writing in the first person to make this biography seem like a memoir, film producer Jim Proser admiringly recreates the life and war experiences of a main character in HBO's fact-based miniseries *The Pacific*.

Yenne, Bill
Aces High: The Heroic Saga of the Two Top-Scoring Aces of World War II. 2009. Berkley Caliber. 348p. ISBN 9780425219546.

During World War II, Axis and Allied nations mobilized millions of soldiers who fought as units with little opportunity for individuals to determine the outcome of battles. In this type of warfare, fighter pilots, who like medieval knights were able to claim personal victories, were the exception. In this admiring dual biography, author Bill Yenne recounts the actions and lives of the U.S. Army Air Force's top scoring pilots, Dick Bong of Wisconsin (1920–1945) and Tommy McGuire of New Jersey (1920–1945).

On Stage and Screen

Before performers step on the stage or before a camera, they have spent countless hours in rehearsal halls and dressing rooms. They may also have been in photographers' studios, their agent's office, and countless hotels, where they meet the press, dine with colleagues, and try to sleep. Being celebrities may make walking the streets undetected impossible and maintaining relationships and families difficult. Still, acclaim for their performances may make their sacrifices worthwhile. The hectic world of stage and screen is described intimately in the following biographies.

Bianculli, David
Dangerously Funny: The Uncensored Story of the Smothers Brothers Comedy Hour. 2009. Simon & Schuster. 392p. ISBN 9781439101162. ⬥

Comic folksingers Tom Smothers (1937–) and Dick Smothers (1939–) really are brothers, unlike many famous comedy acts. After their father's death in World War II, which left them poor and occasionally in the care of relatives, the brothers were always close and supportive of each other. It was natural that the mischievous boys would try music and comedy together. In this story focused on the brothers' three groundbreaking seasons on network television, media critic David Bianculli recounts how they came of age professionally and politically while testing the limits of censorship.

Goudsouzian, Aram
Sidney Poitier: Man, Actor, Icon. 2004. University of North Carolina Press. 480p. ISBN 0807828432.

Celebrated actor Sidney Poitier (1927–) made his mark in Hollywood by playing virtuous African American characters preserving their dignity despite racial injustice. His role in the civil rights movement was praised through its early years, but after the assassination of Martin Luther King, his reserve and belief in nonviolence were questioned by blacks demanding immediate equality. With critical accounts of all the major Poitier films, historian Aram Goudsouzian describes the accomplished actor's life on and off screen through troubled times.

Holroyd, Michael
A Strange Eventful History: The Dramatic Lives of Ellen Terry, Henry Irving, and Their Remarkable Families. 2009. Farrar, Straus and Giroux. 620p. ISBN 9780374270803.

In late Victorian England, contemporaries Ellen Terry (1847–1923) and Henry Irving (1838–1905) were leading players on the London stage. Terry was also the model for paintings by G. F. Watts and John Singer Sargent, while Irving posed for James McNeill Whistler. Acclaimed biographer Michael Holroyd recreates the prestigious world of Victorian Theater in this classic story of two influential actors and their descendents.

Kavanagh, Julie
Nureyev: The Life. 2007. Pantheon Books. 782p. ISBN 9780375405136.

The life of dancer Rudolf Nureyev (1938–1993) was filled with drama from the moment of his birth on a troop train carrying Soviet soldiers and their families to the Manchurian border. Showing great skill in ballet, he received many privileges from Soviet authorities from an early age, but he longed for the wealth and freedom available in Paris, London, and New York. His 1961 defection at the height of the Cold War was international front-page news. In this intimate biography, dancer Julie Kavanagh chronicles Nureyev's acclaimed career and turbulent private life.

Kellow, Brian
▶ *Ethel Merman: A Life*. 2007. Viking. 326p. ISBN 9780670018291.

Broadway actress Ethel Merman (1908–1984) was known for her powerful voice and broad humor. She made her mark as a leading lady in the Cole Porter musicals of the 1930s, becoming as popular as comic stars Bob Hope and Eddie Cantor. Merman skillfully made the transition to movies and then television but often returned to the stage throughout her long career. Author Brian Kellow recreates six decades of stage history in his intimate biography of one of Broadway's best loved stars.

Morley, Sheridan
John Gielgud: The Authorized Biography. 2002. Simon & Schuster. 528p. ISBN 0743222423.

Acting was John Gielgud's life (1904–2000). At 11, he was a sailor in *H.M.S. Pinafore*. Eighty-five years later, he was the protagonist in *Beckett on Film*. Between those productions, he was one of the most influential actors on the British stage. He was even credited with inventing radio theater for the BBC. In this authorized but still candid biography, theater critic Sheridan Morley recounts the long life and career of a shy man who knew everyone important during a century of British stage and screen.

Robb, Brian J.
Heath Ledger: Hollywood's Darkest Star. 2008. Plexus. 207p. ISBN 9780859654272.

 In 10 short years, actor Heath Ledger (1979–2008) transformed his image from an Australian teen soap opera star into a serious internationally known artist willing to take difficult roles. A few bad reviews and broken relationships marred his record, but directors and producers were impressed with his work. Intensely critical of himself, he was addicted to sleeping pills. In this sympathetic and highly illustrated review of Ledger's career and life, celebrity biographer Brian J. Robb celebrates the actor's achievements while mourning his early death.

Turan, Kenneth
Free for All: Joe Papp, the Public, and the Greatest Theater Story Ever Told. 2009. Doubleday. 593p. ISBN 9780767931687.

 Born in Brooklyn, Joseph Papp (1921–1991) produced and directed many influential plays and musicals on and off Broadway, including *True West*, *A Chorus Line*, and *Hair*. In the process, he also fostered the careers of many great actors, including George C. Scott, Meryl Streep, and Kevin Kline. His greatest accomplishment, however, may have been the creation of the public theater in New York and the city's Shakespeare Festival, which draws thousands of people to Central Park annually. In this unique oral history, drama and film critic Kenneth Turan weaves together the memories of many of Papp's colleagues to describe the brilliant but irascible director and recreate the exhilarating world of New York theater.

From Cabarets to Concert Halls

 The world of music inhabits exceptional spaces as varied as the sounds of different instruments. A few quiet notes from a harpsichord may evoke a Baroque era palace, and the brassy sound of a trombone may suggest a smoky 1930s dance hall. Specific rhythms call to mind cities, such as New York, Detroit, or Los Angeles. In this short catalog of musicians' biographies, authors take readers back in time to these places to discover the histories of standard tunes on our constant playlists.

Amburn, Ellis
Buddy Holly: A Biography. 1995. St. Martin's Press. 422p. ISBN 0312134460.

 How did Buddy Holly (1936–1959), a poor skinny boy from Lubbock, Texas, wearing black eyeglasses, become a teen idol? How did he write the hit songs "That'll Be the Day" and "Peggy Sue"? How did he change the world of popular music? Revealing the rebellious side of the young singer once considered a juvenile delinquent, biographer Ellis Amburn chronicles the rapid rise of an ambitious musician in the hardscrabble early days of rock and roll.

Levinson, Peter J.

▶ *Tommy Dorsey: Livin' in a Great Big Way*. 2005. DaCapo Press. 354p. ISBN 0306811111.

Slugging it out with friends and enemies alike was common in the coal-mining towns of Pennsylvania from which trombonist Tommy Dorsey (1905–1956) emerged with his brother saxophonist Jimmy Dorsey. Playing in speakeasies and nightclubs, up until dawn, traveling with big bands, Dorsey publicly hid his combative nature behind sweet swinging melodies. After playing with many headline entertainers, both brothers formed their own bands. Tommy hired young Frank Sinatra as his singer. In this candid biography of a music legend, Peter J. Levinson tells a story filled with sibling rivalry, Hollywood fame, and self-destruction.

Mercer-Taylor, Peter

The Life of Mendelssohn. 2000. Cambridge University Press. 238p. ISBN 0521630258.

Felix Mendelssohn (1809–1847) was a complete musician, talented as a composer, performer, conductor, critic, and scholar. Not only did he impress audiences across Europe with his own music, he also championed the forgotten works of Bach, Mozart, and Beethoven. In this quick-reading title from the Cambridge University Press's *Musical Lives* series, author Peter Mercer-Taylor recreates the world in which Mendelssohn's career was limited only by anti-Semitic prejudice and ill health.

Patoski, Joe Nick

Selena: Como la Flor. 1996. Little, Brown and Company. 291p. ISBN 0316693782.

The musical career of Tejano singer Selena (1971–1995) began at eight on a stage built by her father in Papa Gayo's, her family's Mexican restaurant in Lake Jackson, Texas. It tragically ended at 23 in a parking lot when she was shot after accusing the president of her fan club of theft. According to *Texas Monthly* editor Joe Nick Patoski, Selena's short but eventful life rejuvenated Tex-Mex music and stirred the pride of Hispanic women nationally.

Ribowsky, Mark

Signed, Sealed, and Delivered: The Soulful Journey of Stevie Wonder. 2010. John Wiley & Sons. 337p. ISBN 9780470481509.

Detroit was the birthplace of Motown Records and Stevie Wonder (1950–), who recorded his first hit song at 12, quite an accomplishment for a poor boy blinded in infancy. After his boy genius phase, he became one of the company's biggest stars with 34 top-10 hits and frequent television appearances. Like many stars who became suddenly rich and famous, he overindulged in luxuries, sex, and drugs, losing direction and self-respect. In this frank biography, journalist Mark Ribowsky tells how Wonder, who now collaborates with musicians from many backgrounds, rebuilt his life and rediscovered his musical drive.

Richmond, Peter
Fever: The Life and Music of Miss Peggy Lee. **2006**. Henry Holt. 449p. ISBN 9780805073836. ☙

Glamour, artistry, and sensuality were the trademarks of jazz singer Peggy Lee (1920–2002), who at the height of her popularity was ranked with Louis Armstrong, Frank Sinatra, and Bing Crosby as, to use the author's analogy, the Mount Rushmore of popular music. Through the 1950s and 1960s, she often performed in night clubs and on television, but she nearly disappeared from public view during the rock revolution. After lean years during which she made poor artistic choices, her career rebounded. Peter Richmond's biography of Lee includes accounts of the jazz stage and high society with a dose of gossip.

Secrest, Meryle
Leonard Bernstein: A Life. 1994. Alfred A. Knopf. 471p. ISBN 0679407316.

When Leonard Bernstein (1918–1990) assumed the position of principal conductor of the New York Philharmonic in 1958, American concertgoers cheered. The European hold on major concert halls was broken by a former American prodigy who had impressed music lovers as performer, composer, and conductor. Bernstein then used his fame to promote classical music through innovative radio and television concerts. With much admiration, biographer Meryle Secrest recounts the professional and personal life of a key cultural figure of the 20th century.

Vaughan, Andrew
The Eagles: An American Band. 2010. Sterling. 288p. ISBN 9781402777127.

Country rock was not doing well when the Eagles formed in 1971. Even the Byrds had failed to sell the country sound to a public hungry for hard rock and spectacle. Despite the challenge, four well-traveled musicians fresh from backing Linda Ronstadt started a California-style country band. In this heavily illustrated group biography filled with period details, music critic Andrew Vaughan recounts how the Eagles fought and partied their way to the top of the Billboard charts, dissolved, and, after reforming for an anniversary tour, became the masters of arena rock.

In the Artist's Studio

Artists live outside the mainstream, seeking solitude and good light in which to work, never punching the nine-to-five clock. Inspiration can come at any time. By choosing the artist's life, they may risk poverty if their works are rejected and criticism even when they sell their pieces. Their only friends may be other artists or their patrons, and they may die in obscurity, only to be discovered posthumously. The following books illustrate the worlds of Michelangelo, Mary Cassatt, Dorothea Lange, and other artists whose visions have influenced the way we view their times and our own.

Adams, Henry
Tom and Jack: The Intertwined Lives of Thomas Hart Benton and Jackson Pollock. 2009. Bloomsbury. 405p. ISBN 9781596914209.

Today's museum visitors might never guess that there was any connection between mural painter Thomas Hart Benton (1889–1975) and abstract expressionist Jackson Pollock (1912–1956). The younger artist's work seemed to be a rejection of that of the older man. American art scholar Henry Adams, however, reveals that Benton was Pollock's instructor and mentor, a sort of father figure for the troubled Pollock. How Pollock repaid kindness with a mixture of admiration and disdain is a heartrending story.

Burke, Carolyn
Lee Miller: A Life. 2005. Knopf. 426p. ISBN 0375401474.

After a career as a model for Man Ray, Pablo Picasso, and Edward Steichen, and then success as a surrealist photographer, Lee Miller (1907–1977) covered World War II for *Vogue*. With a distinctive eye for composition, she captured images of combat, the death camps, and life on the home front. After the war, she became a mother, chef, and friend of James Beard. John Phillips described her as "an American free spirit wrapped in the body of a Greek goddess." Author Carolyn Burke portrays Miller as a passionate woman, independent yet talented at collaboration, who held her secrets close.

Gordon, Linda
Dorothea Lange: A Life beyond Limits. 2009. W. W. Norton. 536p. ISBN 9780393057300.

Though a few of her photographs from the Great Depression were well-known and influenced Civil Rights Era photographers, Dorothea Lange (1895–1965) was nearly anonymous at the time of her death. Her early studio photographs, environmental studies, and series on working-class people during and after World War II were mostly forgotten. In death, her reputation has grown without revealing much about the woman behind the camera. In this admiring biography, historian Linda Gordon recounts Lange's life as an artful photographer documenting the drama of her time.

Haverstock, Mary Sayre
George Bellows: An Artist in Action. 2007. Merrell. 160p. ISBN 9781858943930.

George Bellows's (1882–1925) love of art germinated on Sunday afternoons, when the good Methodists of Columbus, Ohio, were required to abstain from any work or unholy activities. Not able to play with friends, he drew and painted on scraps of paper, an activity that his mother allowed. He developed the talent of suggesting action on paper and at 23 moved to New York to seek his fortune. In this attractively illustrated art book, Mary Sayre Haverstock tells how the gregarious Bellows tested the limits of public tolerance with his drawings and paintings of disturbing urban scenes until his tragic death from appendicitis at 43.

Howard, Hugh

The Painter's Chair: George Washington and the Making of American Art. 2009. Bloomsbury. 297p. ISBN 978596912441. ➾

In colonial America and the Early Republic, the most honored and prosperous artists were the painters of portraits. The prize assignment, which would attract many customers and open a market for reprints, was painting George Washington, the general who led the colonists to victory and became the country's first president. Surprisingly, the practical and busy hero was quite accommodating. In this entertaining collective biography, Hugh Howard recounts the lives of the handful of lucky and talented men who won Washington as their subject.

King, Ross

▶ *Michelangelo and the Pope's Ceiling*. 2003. Walker. 373p. ISBN 0802713955. ♜

In 16th-century Rome, the pope was the leading patron of the arts, able to demand work from the city's artists, including Michelangelo Buonarroti (1475–1564). In 1508, Pope Julius II chose Michelangelo to paint the ceiling of the Vatican's Sistine Chapel despite the artist's lack of experience with fresco painting. The proud but cash-strapped Michelangelo tested the pope's patience and tolerance with delays and unauthorized designs. Art historian Ross King tells the artist's dramatic story against the backdrop of war, plague, and religious turmoil.

Mathews, Nancy Mowll

Mary Cassatt: A Life. 1994. Villard. 383p. ISBN 039458497X.

Born into a wealthy banking family in Pennsylvania and educated while her family toured Europe, Mary Cassatt (1844–1926) spent most of her adult life in France where she was included in the salon of the impressionist painters. Quietly she focused her life on drawing and painting women and children from many backgrounds. In this older book with many black-and-white illustrations, Cassatt-expert Nancy Mowll Mathews recounts how a Victorian-era woman who never married defied rules of gender and culture to become an intellectual elite.

Richardson, John

Sacred Monsters, Sacred Masters: Beaton, Capote, Dalí, Picasso, Freud, Warhol, and More. 2001. Random House. 363p. ISBN 0679424903.

Art critic John Richardson seems to have a low opinion of most people, especially artists, their friends, and the patrons who support them. He cheerfully calls them drunkards, liars, and thieves. Ironically, the critic seems to love their stories and the art they create. In this collection of irreverent biographical sketches, Richardson recreates the mad world of 20th-century art.

Inside the World of Books

Novelists and other writers do not create something of nothing. Although their books may not be factual, they still must, like historians and biographers, infuse their writings with psychological truth that reflects human experience. Understandably, they draw their characters, stories, and settings from their own lives. Often, the most talented writers have emerged from troubled times and have found the pleasure of their literary success fleeting, as shown in these eight biographies.

Briggs, Julia
Virginia Woolf: An Inner Life. 2005. Harcourt. 528p. ISBN 0151011435.

English novelist and essayist Virginia Woolf (1882–1941) lived in and for her books. Much of the evidence is in her diaries and letters, which began to document the creative process eight years before the 1915 publication of *The Voyage Out*. Publishing 16 books in 26 years, her thoughts were more often with her books than on her relationships and daily life. Yet, she was still acutely aware of social discord and political injustice. In this literary biography, Woolf scholar Julia Briggs carefully shows how book by book the unsettled novelist directed her experiences into her fiction and commentaries.

Byrne, Paula
Mad World: Evelyn Waugh and the Secrets of Brideshead. 2010. Harper. 367p. ISBN 9780060881306.

Despite the protestations by novelist Evelyn Waugh (1903–1966) that *Brideshead Revisited* is not autobiographical, the fictional family in the book resembles his friends the Lygons who lived in opulence in their great house Madresfield, called Mad by the wayward son Hugh Lygon. Waugh's circumstances also resembled those of his character Charles Ryder. In this slice-of-life biography, author Paula Byrne examines how life shapes literature and the impact of one book on an author's life.

Davis, Linda H.
▶ *Badge of Courage: The Life of Stephen Crane*. 1998. Houghton Mifflin. 414p. ISBN 0899199348. ☙

American author Stephen Crane (1871–1900) was in constant motion during his short life, traveling, meeting famous people, and writing five novels, three short story collections, two volumes of poetry, and essays for many magazines. Handsome, charming, and ambitious, he quickly impressed publishers, editors, and literary figures in the United States and Great Britain, but he also neglected his finances, wife, and health. Sadly, his death from consumption was probably preventable. Linda H. Davis's biography of Crane is a lament for life tragically lost.

Delbanco, Andrew
Melville: His World and Work. 2005. Alfred A. Knopf. 415p. ISBN 0375403140.

The acclaim for the novels of former seaman Herman Melville (1819–1981) dipped decisively during the 15 years of his active literary career. After the warm reception of his lighter-hearted early novels *Typee* and *Omoo*, Melville turned darker with each new work, believing readers would follow. *Moby Dick* sold particularly poorly, and Melville eventually became a customs agent to support his family. In this sympathetic literary biography, author Andrew Delbanco recounts how Melville withstood public scorn, retreated for a period of several decades, and then late in life began afresh by writing his masterpiece *Billy Budd*.

Loncraine, Rebecca
The Real Wizard of Oz: The Life and Times of L. Frank Baum. 2009. Gotham Books. 329p. ISBN 9781592404490. ⊋

Before L. Frank Baum (1856–1919) wrote *The Wonderful Wizard of Oz* in 1899, he struggled to find his place and occupation. Then, inspired by the World Columbian Exposition in Chicago in 1893, the natural storyteller wrote a clever tale about a magical city where a young girl, a scarecrow, a tin man, and a lion found whatever they had lost. American readers responded enthusiastically, claiming the Oz stories as their own modern fairy tales. In this sympathetic literary biography, Rebecca Loncraine tells how Baum became the increasingly reluctant voice of Oz.

Meade, Marion
Lonelyhearts: The Screwball World of Nathanael West and Eileen McKenney. 2010. Houghton Mifflin Harcourt. 392p. ISBN 9780151011490.

Nathanael West (1903–1940) sold few of his darkly comic novels during his lifetime. Eileen McKenney (1913–1940) was known as the heroine of her sister Ruth's lighthearted book *My Sister Eileen*. When they met, the couple had common literary friends in New York and Hollywood but little else in common. In this atmospheric dual biography, literary historian Marion Meade recounts the lives of the madcap couple cut short by a car accident that seemed inevitable to their friends, including authors Sidney J. Perelman and Bennett Cerf.

Sisman, Adam
Boswell's Presumptuous Task: The Making of the Life of Dr. Johnson. 2000. Farrar, Straus and Giroux. 351p. ISBN 0374115613. ⅄

After lexicographer Samuel Johnson defined in an essay how modern biography should be written, his close friend James Boswell (1740–1795) inherited the task of writing the first example, the book to guide future biographers. The subject was Johnson himself. Though Boswell had prepared by observing and recording his friend's words for 21 years, he struggled for another 7 years to write the landmark book. In this biography of a biographer, author Adam Sisman recreates a time when the world of literature was transformed.

Spurling, Hilary
Pearl Buck in China: Journey to the Good Earth. 2010. Simon & Schuster. 304p. ISBN 9781416540427.

    The daughter of missionaries who often left her in the company of the cook or a tutor, novelist Pearl Buck (1892–1973) did not realize that she was not Chinese until age eight when her family fled almost certain death during the Boxer Rebellion. Having been raised in two traditions, Buck always longed to return to China while touring in the West, seeking aid and sympathy for her war-torn adopted land. In this literary biography, award-winning biographer Hilary Spurling eloquently recounts how Buck's love of China was ever in her thoughts and stories.

With Beakers or Binoculars

    The advancement of science requires collaboration, so being accepted in a community of peers is enormously important to men and women of science. Advanced degrees, however, do not guarantee the good behavior of their bearers, and research institutions are notorious for reflecting the prejudices of their societies. Scientists may make great sacrifices to study at great universities or in the field, as shown by these biographies.

Brown, G.I.
Scientist, Soldier, Statesman, Spy: Count Rumford: The Extraordinary Life of a Scientific Genius. 1999. Sutton Publishing. 182p. ISBN 0750921846.

    In the 18th and early 19th centuries, science was mostly conducted by gentlemen who also had other pursuits, such as running the affairs of state and entertaining their peers. Such a man was Benjamin Thompson (1753–1814), a colonist who fled America when he was exposed as a British spy. By misrepresenting his lineage, he became a British statesman and then was dubbed a count in Bavaria. His passion was experimenting with heat and light. A little science background helps reading this engaging biography.

Goldsmith, Barbara
Obsessive Genius: The Inner World of Marie Curie. 2005. W. W. Norton. 256p. ISBN 0393051374.

    Although Polish chemist Marie Curie (1867–1934) studied radioactivity, discovered radium and polonium, invented a mobile X-ray machine, and won Nobel Prizes in both chemistry and physics, she gained little respect from contemporaries. Her work was often ignored by the men of science, and her many firsts for scientific women were discounted. Only her collaboration with her beloved husband Pierre opened opportunities for further research. In this quick-reading biography, author Barbara Goldsmith recounts the intensely dramatic personal and professional struggle of a brilliant woman.

Hirschfeld, Alan
The Electric Life of Michael Faraday. 2006. Walker & Company. 258p. ISBN 0802714706.

Too poor for college, bookbinding apprentice Michael Faraday (1791–1867) learned about science and nature from the old volumes that his master was binding. Using common tools and materials, he rigged his own experiments to test what he learned. In this admiring biography with a bit of science fact, physics professor Alan Hirschfeld describes how inventing an electric generator and a motor allowed an amateur scientist to join the ranks of England's eminent scientists and become a friend of Charles Dickens.

Maddox, Brenda
Rosalind Franklin: The Dark Lady of DNA. 2002. HarperCollins. 380p. ISBN 0060184078.

Rosalind Franklin (1920–1958) was a respected microbiologist with many friends in her field, yet colleague James Watson attacked her work as mediocre. Ironically, Watson and Francis Crick relied heavily on Franklin's research findings and her photographs of DNA in their celebrated *The Double Helix*. In this sympathetic account, biographer Brenda Maddox restores the reputation of a brilliant scientist and amateur mountain climber who should be acclaimed for her breakthroughs on DNA.

Quammen, David
The Reluctant Mr. Darwin: An Intimate Portrait of Charles Darwin and the Making of His Theory of Evolution. 2006. Norton. 304p. ISBN 978 0393059816.

Charles Darwin (1809–1882) was a cautious man who studied nature very carefully before issuing reports and formulating theories. He knew that his theory of evolution would upset many of his colleagues and trouble his religious wife. In this intimate biography, David Quammen chronicles the scientist's quiet years spent away from London, the time when Darwin prepared to publish *On the Origin of Species*, a book that is still both highly praised and condemned.

Repcheck, Jack
▶ *Copernicus' Secret: How the Scientific Revolution Began*. 2007. Simon & Schuster. 239p. ISBN 9780743289511.

Roman Catholic cleric Nicholas Copernicus (1473–1543) was a late bloomer with little personal ambition. In an age when most scholars entered universities at 14 and finished in 3 years, he started at 19 and attended for 12, finally earning a degree in canon law. He was only an amateur astronomer but understood mathematics and calculated the orbits of planets. In this quick-reading book focusing on the cleric's final years, author Jack Repcheck tells how

Copernicus finally dared to publish *On the Revolution of Heavenly Spheres*, the book that shook the foundation of his church and began a battle for observable evidence replacing Biblical scriptures in scientific proofs.

Smith, Jane S.

The Garden of Invention: Luther Burbank and the Business of Breeding Plants. 2009. Penguin Press. 354p. ISBN 9781594202094.

In 1905, the California State Board of Trade threw a lavish testimonial dinner to celebrate the contributions of master plant breeder Luther Burbank (1849–1926) to the economy of their state. Typical of the time, Burbank and the public saw nothing but good in the scientific management and industrialization of agriculture. In her examination of Burbank's career, science historian Jane S. Smith takes readers back to a time when he was admired as the world's most famous gardener and a champion of progress equal to Alexander Graham Bell and Thomas Edison.

Todd, Kim

Chrysalis: Maria Sibylla Merian and the Secrets of Metamorphosis. 2007. Harcourt Inc. 328p. ISBN 9780151011087. ⧗

As a child, Maria Sibylla Merian (1647–1717) learned from her stepfather, the still life painter Jacob Marrel, how to draw and paint insects, especially moths and butterflies. Then she spent many years as a wife and mother, delaying her quest to become an amateur naturalist. Kim Todd recounts how the so-called Mother of Lepidopterology left her family and comfortable life to sail to Surinam at 52 and spend 2 years alone studying and illustrating the flora and fauna of the South American rainforest.

In the Court of the King and Queen

Life in royal courts with crowds of ambitious people around the monarchs has always been filled with drama, intrigue, jealousy, infidelity, insanity, and sometimes magnificence. The fortunes of individuals rise and fall with the favor of the king or queen. The books in this list tell the stories of cabinet members, ladies-in-waiting, princesses, and others who might either receive great bounty or lose their heads.

Buckley, Veronica

The Secret Wife of Louis XIV: Françoise d'Abigné, Madame de Maintenon. 2009. Farrar, Straus and Giroux. 498p. ISBN 9780374158309.

When Louis XIV of France fell in love with Françoise d'Abigné (1635–1719), she was a widow serving as a governess to the king's royal favorite. Truly smitten, the Catholic king forsook his other mistress and gave Françoise the title Madame de Maintenon, upsetting his ministers who believed that his highness would be mocked for consorting with a Huguenot born in prison. In this historical biography, Veronica Buckley recreates the splendid but dangerous court of the Sun King.

Budiansky, Stephen
Her Majesty's Spymaster: Elizabeth I, Sir Francis Walsingham, and the Birth of Modern Espionage. 2005. Viking. 235p. ISBN 0670034266. ≷

Was Sir Francis Walsingham (1530?–1590), principal secretary and privy councilor under Queen Elizabeth I, as ruthless as he is portrayed in modern dramas? Historian Stephen Budiansky thinks not, believing that Walsingham was a loyal and devoted servant who would kill for his queen when necessary but who also was a serious Puritan with an ethical code that he closely followed. In this account of Walsingham's life at court, the author shows how the spymaster worked carefully under the queen's ever-changing foreign policy to identify assassins and invaders.

Fox, Julia
▶ *Jane Boleyn: The True Story of the Infamous Lady Rochford*. 2007. Ballantine Books. 379p. ISBN 9780345485410.

Sometimes, the story of momentous affairs is vividly told from the perspective of a fringe character. Such is the case for Jane Boleyn (1505–1542), the sister-in-law to Anne Boleyn, the second wife of Henry VIII of England. Jane saw both her husband and Anne executed, yet she survived to become lady-in-waiting to Henry's next three wives. Tudor historian Julia Fox recounts Jane's extravagant life at court in this historical biography with a particularly colorful section of illustrations.

Gelardi, Julia P.
In Triumph's Wake: Royal Mother, Tragic Daughters, and the Price They Paid for Glory. 2008. St. Martin's Press. 404p. ISBN 9780312371050.

Pity the daughter whose mother was a mighty queen. Being as potent a monarch was too much to ask. Giving readers a peek inside courts across Europe from the end of the Renaissance to the modern age, historian Julia P. Gelardi recounts the tragic stories of Queen Isabella of Castile and her daughter Catherine of Aragon, Empress Maria Theresa of Austria and her daughter Marie Antoinette, and Queen Victoria of Great Britain and her daughter Empress Frederick.

Morgan, Susan
Bombay Anna: The Real Story and Remarkable Adventures of the King and I Governess. 2008. University of California Press. 274p. ISBN 9780520252264.

Anna Leonowens (1831–1915) was not as ladylike as depicted in the musical *The King and I*. She wrote critically about her experiences in her memoir *The English Governess in the Siamese Court*. Using Leonowens's original observations and other sources, author Susan Morgan recreates the life of a world traveler and the exotic court of the King of Siam.

Tyldesley, Joyce
Cleopatra: Last Queen of Egypt. 2008. Basic Books. 290p. ISBN 9780465009404.
　　Because Alexander the Great established the Ptolemies as rulers over Egypt, Cleopatra VI (69–30 BCE) has often been classified as a foreigner by Egyptologists. Historian Joyce Tyldesley argues, however, that the family that ruled from Alexandria for 300 years embraced Egyptian customs and religion, and Cleopatra strove to be the traditional queen as goddess and mother of her land. As co-ruler with first her brothers and then her son, she strove to keep her court viable through shrewd alliances with powerful Romans, Julius Caesar and Marc Antony. Rejecting many myths, Tyldesley profiles the historical queen as an accomplished leader and the last true Egyptian monarch.

Weber, Caroline
Queen of Fashion: What Marie Antoinette Wore to the Revolution. 2006. Henry Holt. 412p. ISBN 9780805079494. ☙
　　In the court of Louis XVI of France were many people employed by the fashion-conscious queen, Marie Antoinette (1755–1793). Seamstresses, laundresses, and dressers worked to keep the queen in lavish dresses that proved to be a great insult to the French public, most of whom were poor. In this cultural biography, Caroline Weber recounts the rise and fall of an insensitive queen, with many stories about her controversial wardrobe.

Weir, Alison
Mistress of the Monarchy: The Life of Katherine Swynford, Duchess of Lancaster. 2009. Ballantine Books. 392p. ISBN 9780345453235.
　　Katherine Swynford (1350?–1403), wife of John of Gaunt, lived during the reigns of Richard II and Henry IV of England, a period filled with war, plague, and rebellion. Noted novelist and biographer Alison Weir claims that she decided as a young girl to write about Swynford when she read Anya Seton's novel *Katherine*. Nearly 40 years later, after writing many other books about medieval characters, Weir wrote this love story about a woman who defied social customs, controlled her own destiny, and married the man of her dreams.

In High Society

　　People with money and social status receive many invitations: come to the ball, join our club, or spend a weekend on the yacht. They live on estates, know elegant people, and take the grandest vacations. Their opportunities are vast, if only they can navigate past the dangers of arrogance and vanity. Most importantly, they have to maintain their standing. The following eight biographies are set in mansions and penthouses of the rich where the character of the upper class is tested.

Flanders, Judith
Circle of Sisters: Alice Kipling, Georgiana Burne-Jones, Agnes Poynter and Louisa Baldwin. 2005. W. W. Norton. 392p. ISBN 0393052109.

Though the British class system has been thought to be very rigid for centuries, author Judith Flanders shows that it has in fact been somewhat fluid. Four daughters of modest Methodist minister George Browne Macdonald (1805–1868) married into the upper classes and helped shape the empire through their offspring. In this family biography, the author recounts the success and distress in the lives of these remarkable women.

Flem, Lydia
Casanova: The Man Who Really Loved Women. 1997. Farrar, Straus, Giroux. 256p. ISBN 0374119570. ➲

Now known as one of history's greatest lover, Giacomo Casanova (1725–1798) would be amused by his narrowly focused reputation. He was considered in his time to be a great poet, playwright, lyricist, historian, and polymath, not to mention soldier, priest, and con artist. He knew everyone of importance in Venice, Paris, Prague, and St. Petersburg. In his epic *History of My Life*, Casanova thoroughly documented social life in Europe before the Age of Revolution. Lydia Flem recounts the life and observations of a rogue with an honest streak in this entertaining biography.

Gordon, Lois
Nancy Cunard: Heiress, Muse, Political Idealist. 2007. Columbia University Press. 447p. ISBN 9780231139380.

With both beauty and wealth, shipping heiress Nancy Cunard (1896–1965) could live a life of the luxurious idle. As a young woman, she posed for painters and photographers and entertained literary figures, including T. S. Eliot, Ernest Hemingway, and Pablo Neruda. In time, however, she adopted many progressive causes, such as social justice and international relief, spurring her to become a poet, publisher, war correspondent, and relief worker. In this admiring biography, Lois Gordon chronicles the transformation of a socialite into a humanitarian.

Graham, Lawrence Otis
The Senator and the Socialite: The True Story of America's First Black Dynasty. 2006. HarperCollins. 455p. ISBN 9780060184124.

Former slave Blanche Kelso Bruce (1841–1898) of Mississippi was the first African American to serve a complete six-year term in the U.S. Senate. He married Josephine Beal Willson (1841–1923), daughter of aristocratic blacks from Philadelphia. Together they enjoyed the power and high society of Washington and Harlem for decades. Their son Roscoe excelled at Harvard and befriended John D. Rockefeller, Jr. With the third generation, however, the family fortunes failed. In this multigenerational biography, historian Lawrence Otis Graham recounts the lives of a black family trying to thrive in a white society.

Jacob, Kathryn Allamong

King of the Lobby: The Life and Times of Sam Ward, Man-about-Washington in the Gilded Age. 2010. John Hopkins University Press. 212p. ISBN 9780801893971.

Fourth son of a wealthy New York family, Samuel Ward (1814–1884) had already failed as a gold miner and businessman when he arrived in the District of Columbia in 1859 as a secret representative of the government of Paraguay. Known for his friendship with the poet Henry Wadsworth Longfellow and as brother of Julia Ward Howe, he charmed his way into social circles and began hosting dinners for congressmen. By the 1880s, he was the most powerful lobbyist in Washington. In this short entertaining biography, historian Kathryn Allamong Jacob profiles the man who transformed lobbying from bribe-giving to more subtle offers of power and wealth.

Kelly, Ian

▶ *Beau Brummell: The Ultimate Man of Style*. 2006. Free Press. 393p. ISBN 9780743270892. ☙

That Beau Brummell (1778–1840) was born in an apartment on Downing Street in London was a testament to his father's ambition. That he died in an asylum was a tragedy of his own making. He had been best man at the wedding of the Prince of Wales, been schooled at Eton and Oxford, and been the model for Lord Byron's *Don Juan*. Always a man of fashion, Brummell had also led men to abandon stockings for pants and short coats. With an eye for detail, actor and author Ian Kelly tells a story of self-destruction in early 19th-century high society.

Love, Robert

The Great Oom: The Improbable Birth of Yoga in America. 2010. Viking. 402p. ISBN 9780670021758.

For introducing the British-banned practice of yoga to wealthy followers in the United States, Dr. Pierre Bernard (1876–1955), sometimes called the Great Oom, was labeled as a charlatan and subversive. Through a concerted campaign, religious leaders, government officials, and newspaper editors nearly ruined the reputation of the entrepreneur of health, who had been born Perry Arnold Baker in Iowa. Setting his story among the rich and influential classes from the Gilded Age to the sexual revolution, journalist Robert Love shows how Bernard persisted and thrived to eventually become a rich man considered the Father of American Yoga.

Shand-Tucci, Douglass

The Art of Scandal: The Life and Times of Isabella Stewart Gardner. 1997. HarperCollins. 351p. ISBN 0060186437.

By turning her distinctive mansion into an art museum frozen in time and dictating that no piece of art could ever be moved, Boston's Isabella Stewart Gardner (1840–1924) tried to establish forever a legacy for which she would be remembered. She also burned all her letters to erase evidence of her love affairs and the provenance of her art acquisitions. According to author Douglass Shand-Tucci, Gardner was too well known by artists, authors, and the cream of New England society to cleanse her reputation. In this intimate biography, the author recounts the life of an intractable woman that Boston will never forget.

Chapter Four

Language

How do biographers attract readers to their books? Sometimes *how* they say it is as crucial as *what* they say. Some readers may be attracted by the promise of a biography that reads like a novel or the novelty of a life described through essays instead of through chronological chapters. They may prefer short books that recount key events from a life, or they may savor an epic biography that tells everything and takes weeks to read. Some readers enjoy exposés, while others prefer books that defend fallen heroes. Sometimes, an oversized tribute full of pictures and a few well-chosen words is what catches a reader's eye.

The ways that biographers tell their stories are many. Valerie Martin presents the life of Saint Francis of Assisi through a series of acts, with each scene resembling a Renaissance painting depicting a key event in the saint's life. In his epic biography about Alexander Hamilton, Ron Chernow recounts the Founding Father's life in great detail from his birth in the West Indies to his death from a bullet shot by his enemy Aaron Burr. Bill Minutaglio and W. Michael Smith use quotations frequently in their tribute to their journalistic colleague Molly Ivins. In his photobiography about Kurt Cobain, Charles R. Cross uses the rock star's own paintings and drawings along with many photographs to illustrate a desperate life that ended in suicide.

In this chapter are nine book lists, the first three of which include books that resemble other popular forms of literature: the novel, the short story collection, and the essay collection. The next two lists focus on book length, and the selections may be compared to novellas and epic tales. The sixth and seventh lists feature the authors, who write from the perspective of being investigative journalists or of being friends of the subjects. The final two lists feature biographies built around quotations or photographs.

Episodic Biography

Screenwriters see lives as a series of scenes that can be scripted and produced on film. A few biographers have taken a similar approach, cutting the dull days, months, and even years out of their stories so they can focus on the key events in their subjects' lives. The results are biographies that read much like novels. Here are seven unusual examples featuring the dramatic lives of characters as diverse as composer Frédéric Chopin and Saint Francis of Assisi.

Eisler, Benita

▶ *Chopin's Funeral*. 2003. Knopf. 230p. ISBN 03755409459.

Benita Eisler begins her biography of Polish pianist and composer Frédéric Chopin (1810–1849) with an evocative description of his dramatic funeral in Paris and then flashes back to scenes from his event-filled life. Chopin's exile from Poland, musical genius, long illness, and unusual romance with the French novelist George Sand are recurring themes. Pianist Franz Liszt, painter Eugene Delacroix, novelist Victor Hugo, and other artistic denizens of Paris fill this novel-like biography.

Haley, James L.

Wolf: The Lives of Jack London. 2010. Basic Books. 364p. ISBN 9780465004782.

Born in San Francisco, author Jack London (1876–1916) was an illegitimate child adopted by a loving stepfather but then forced to can pickles in a factory at 14. Like a character from a Dickens novel, he was eager to escape poverty. He tried shoveling coal, seal hunting, prospecting for gold in Alaska, and even oyster piracy before becoming a war correspondent and novelist. In sequential chapters focusing on London's many vocations, biographer James L. Haley recounts each phase of London's unusual life.

Imber, Gerald

Genius on the Edge: The Bizarre Double Life of Dr. William Stewart Halsted. 2010. Kaplan Publishing. 387p. ISBN 9781607146278.

When William Halsted (1852–1922) began his medical studies, surgery was dangerous treatment for any injury or disease. Bleeding or infection killed most surgical patients. The developments of anesthesia and antisepsis transformed medicine, giving Halsted the chance to introduce gallstone removal, hernia repair, and radical mastectomy. The acclaimed Johns Hopkins Hospital surgeon, however, baffled colleagues by occasionally disappearing for months. In 37 episodic chapters, surgeon Gerald Imber reveals how Halsted's experiments with medical uses of cocaine led to an addiction that complicated his career.

Martin, Valerie
Salvation: Scenes from the Life of St. Francis. 2001. Knopf. 268p. ISBN 0375409831.

The image of Saint Francis of Assisi (1182–1226) is one of the most popular in Christian art. The scenes from his life, including meeting the leper on the road, receiving the stigmata, and death surrounded by members of his order, are depicted in countless paintings from the Middle Ages and Renaissance. Author Valerie Martin recounts the life of the Italian saint through a series of episodes that describe these scenes and read like short stories. She starts with his death and takes the readers back in time.

Murphy, Caroline P.
The Pope's Daughter: The Extraordinary Life of Felice della Rovere. 2005. Oxford University Press. 359p. ISBN 9780195182682.

In Renaissance Rome, being a widow had some advantages. When Pope Julius sought to marry off his illegitimate daughter Felice della Rovere (1483–1536) for a second time, she had her own money and vetoed suitors until her father found one rich enough. By the time of her third marriage, she was able to choose her own husband. Art historian Caroline P. Murphy tells through a series of episodes a richly detailed story about a scheming woman whose lust for power and ambition for her sons eventually led to her downfall.

Saunders, Frances Stonor
The Woman Who Shot Mussolini. 2010. Metropolitan Books. 380p. ISBN 9780805091212. ☙

On the morning of April 7, 1926, a middle-aged Anglo-Irish woman stood on the steps of Rome's Palazzo dei Conservatori, waiting for Italian dictator Benito Mussolini to emerge. Though surrounded by police, Violet Gibson (1876–1956) raised a pistol eight inches from the head of her victim and shot, only nicking the dictator's nose. Through a series of short chapters, author Frances Stonor Saunders deftly reconstructs the life of a former debutante who dabbled in Irish nationalism and religious cults.

Todd, Olivier
Albert Camus: A Life. 1998. Alfred A. Knopf. 434p. ISBN 0679428550.

Authors sometimes say they want no biographies; they want only to be known for their work. French novelist and philosopher Albert Camus (1913–1960) said as much while also insisting that his writings were not autobiographical. Literary critic Olivier Todd is among many scholars who reject Camus's statements as a ruse to give his family some privacy. In this biography using Camus's well-kept papers, Todd divides the short conflicted life of the proud novelist into 50 poignant episodes.

Biographical Shorts

Among the many novels on library and bookstore shelves are collections of short stories, giving fiction readers an option to read highly focused, economic narratives that may satisfy their reading interests quickly. Biography shelves accommodate similar volumes that might be called biographical shorts. These books thematically collect short profiles that quickly reveal interesting characters and their remarkable stories. The friends of Abraham Lincoln, the mothers of presidents, and profiles from the *New Yorker* are three of the high-interest topics in these biographical collections.

Angelo, Bonnie
> *First Mothers: The Women Who Shaped the Presidents*. 2000. William Morrow. 451p. ISBN 0688156312.
>
> Every time a new president is elected, newspaper and television feature writers seek to profile his mother. Her pedigree is scrutinized, and she is always asked about her son's childhood (only sons so far) and whether she knew her son was bound for distinction. In this entertaining collective biography, journalist Bonnie Angelo recounts the lives of the mothers of presidents from Franklin D. Roosevelt to Bill Clinton.

Donald, David Herbert
> ▶ *We Are Lincoln Men: Abraham Lincoln and His Friends*. 2003. Simon & Schuster. 269p. ISBN 0743254686. ☙
>
> Though thought to be a genuinely affable man, President Abraham Lincoln developed few close friendships during his life. Noted Lincoln scholar David Herbert Donald believed that only six men could be called confidantes. In this short collection of profiles, Donald recounts how each of these men met and worked with the president who led his country through a terrible civil war.

Gates, Henry Louis, Jr.
> *Faces of America: How 12 Extraordinary People Discovered Their Pasts*. 2010. New York University Press. 277p. ISBN 9780814732649.
>
> How do our ancestors shape our lives? Author Henry Louis Gates Jr. addressed this question by writing genealogical profiles of 12 famous Americans. Believing that the characteristics of people are the sum of their predecessors, Gates used genealogical research and DNA analysis to discover his subjects' diverse origins. Readers learn with the celebrities, including comedian Stephen Colbert, cellist Yo-Yo Ma, and actress Meryl Streep, how their ancestors reside within their genes and hearts.

Kukla, Jon
> *Mr. Jefferson's Women*. 2007. Alfred A. Knopf. 279p. ISBN 9781400043248. ☙
>
> Thomas Jefferson, who penned famous words about the rights of all men, was not a skilled suitor of women. Three Virginia women rejected his romantic

proposals before the fourth accepted. Then, after his much beloved wife died, the woman in his life was one of his slaves. Using documentary evidence, historian Jon Kukla profiles these five women and their relationships with the enigmatic statesman.

McCullough, David

Brave Companions: Portraits in History. 1992. Simon & Schuster. 240p. ISBN 0671792768. ⚉

Known for his epic biographies of presidents, historian David McCullough has also written numerous short profiles of other American historical figures for magazines, such as *American Heritage* and *Smithsonian*. In each of these intimate pieces, the author succinctly dramatizes important American historical events. Naturalist Alexander von Humboldt, novelist Harriet Beecher Stowe, and artist Frederic Remington are among his subjects. McCullough's biographical articles written during the 1970s and the 1980s are brought together in this compelling collection.

Remnick, David, ed.

Life Stories: Profiles from the New Yorker. 2000. Random House. 530p. ISBN 0375503552.

Many of America's most celebrated authors, such as Calvin Trillan, Truman Capote, and Roger Angell, have written biographical profiles of important contemporaries for the *New Yorker*. According to magazine editor David Remnick, these intimate pieces introduced readers to newsmakers of the past century, including politicians, scientists, artists, athletes, and novelists. In this volume, Remnick celebrated his magazine's 75th anniversary by republishing 25 of its most memorable profiles.

Roberts, Steven V.

From Every End of This Earth: 13 Families and the New Lives They Made in America. 2009. Harper. 323p. ISBN 9780061245619.

Coming from Vietnam, El Salvador, India, Rwanda, and many other countries, immigrants have risked their lives and fortunes to immigrate to America. Many thought that the people of the United States would welcome them and readily offer opportunities to become neighbors, but these newcomers instead found prejudice to overcome. In this collection of touching short biographies, journalist Steven V. Roberts shows why he believes brave immigrants should be admired and welcomed into our country.

Eloquent Essays

Most biographers choose to tell their stories chronologically. A rare few prefer to examine their subjects through topical essays. For example, in her book *How to Live—or—A Life of Montaigne in One Question and Twenty Attempts at an Answer*, Sarah Bakewell reveals the life of her subject through

20 essays focusing on Montaigne's own essays. In *Coco Chanel: The Legend and the Life*, Justine Picardie similarly reveals the character of Coco Chanel through essays about clothes, friendship, love, fame, and perfume. The biographical essay model works especially well for books about writers, musicians, and philosophers, as seen in the following list.

Bakewell, Sarah
How to Live—or—A Life of Montaigne in One Question and Twenty Attempts at an Answer. 2010. Other Press. 389p. ISBN 9781590514252.

Michel Eyquem de Montaigne (1533–1592) is recognized by many as the first memoirist to write thoughtful essays about his daily life instead of recounting achievements. According to biographer Sarah Bakewell, Montaigne took great care to examine and express his feelings, which he wrote and rewrote over the course of 20 years before publishing. In 20 essays, Bakewell closely examines the life of a thinker who inspired many future authors, including Ralph Waldo Emerson, Gustave Flaubert, and Virginia Woolf.

Frykholm, Amy
Julian of Norwich: A Contemplative Biography. 2010. Paraclete Press. 147p. ISBN 9781557256263.

In 14th-century England, when the Roman Catholic Church forbade the use of English in religious texts, an anchorite risked expulsion by quietly defying her superiors. Known to us now as Julian of Norwich (1342–1416), this mysterious woman spent 20 years writing her spiritual visions and her own theological explanations of them, making her the first known woman to write a book in English. Using the text of Julian's *A Revelation of Love* and other medieval texts, journalist Amy Frykholm constructs through essays a life of the legendary mystic.

Malcolm, Janet
Two Lives: Gertrude and Alice. 2007. Yale University Press. 227p. ISBN 9780300125511. ☙

Why did Jewish authors Gertrude Stein (1874–1946) and Alice B. Toklas (1877–1967) decide to stay in Vichy France during World War II? How did these lesbian lovers survive the notice of the intolerant Nazis? Why did they even stay together? Their legendary fights, witnessed by many literary and artistic figures, were bitter and long. In three probing biographical essays, author Janet Malcolm examines the novels, poems, and autobiographical writings of Stein and Toklas, looking for clues to their relationship.

Parekh, Bhikhu
Gandhi. 2010. Sterling. 181p. ISBN 9781402768873.

Indian statesman and spiritual leader Mohandas Karamchand Gandhi (1869–1948) sought *satya* (truth) through *ahimsa* (nonviolence) according to *dharma* (duty or moral law). He failed in his quest to keep India whole after its liberation from Great Britain, but his spiritual teachings influenced oppressed people worldwide. Through seven topical essays, political science professor Bhikhu Parekh recounts Gandhi's life and explains the thoughts of the 20th century's icon of peace.

Picardie, Justine
Coco Chanel: The Legend and the Life. 2010. HarperCollins. 343p. ISBN 9780061963858.

Though French fashion designer Coco Chanel (1883–1971) was born in a poorhouse and raised in an orphanage, she is remembered for the elegance of her dresses and the high society company that she kept. Her studio in Paris remains a destination for cultural pilgrims many decades after her death. Through a series of essays illustrated with photographs and Chanel's own drawings, author Justine Picardie examines many aspects of the designer's life, including her impoverished youth, the development of her fame, her love of a married man, her relations with friends, and the story of her signature perfume.

Watts, Steven
The People's Tycoon: Henry Ford and the American Century. 2005. Alfred A. Knopf. 614p. ISBN 0375407359.

The merits of Henry Ford's life (1863–1947) are a hotly debated historical topic. John D. Rockefeller, Woodrow Wilson, Vladimir Lenin, and Adolf Hitler admired the inventor for statements and actions that drew the condemnation of others. By making each chapter of this biography of Ford an essay on a different aspect of the industrialist's life, historian Steven Watts shows the importance and complexity of a man who was both folk hero and villain in his own time.

Weinstein, Philip
Becoming Faulkner: The Art and Life of William Faulkner. 2010. Oxford University Press. 250p. ISBN 9780195341539.

Faulkner-scholar Philip Weinstein thinks that most biographers have misunderstood Southern novelist William Faulkner (1897–1962). The majority opinion is that the novelist succeeded in literature *despite* his personal problems, whereas Weinstein holds that Faulkner succeeded *because* of his problems. As a result, in his collection of biographical essays, each on a different aspect of Faulkner's troubled life, Weinstein is unapologetic in his admiration of the novelist's achievements.

Wilde, Laurent de
Monk. 1997. Marlowe. 214p. ISBN 1569247404.

Fame did not translate into wealth or even comfort in the case of jazz composer and pianist Thelonious Monk (1917–1982). Thanks to alcohol and drug abuse, Monk was always short of cash and struggled to meet his family obligations. In his final years, he was struck silent by an undiagnosed mental illness. In this collection of essays, jazz pianist and critic Laurent de Wilde examines the life, career, and legacy of a man who was admired by his contemporaries and shaped the future of jazz.

Woolf, Jenny

▶ *The Mystery of Lewis Carroll: Discovering the Whimsical, Thoughtful, and Sometimes Lonely Man Who Created Alice in Wonderland*. 2010. St. Martin's Press. 326p. ISBN 9780312612986.

British journalist Jenny Woolf has been fascinated by the mathematician and poet Charles Lutwidge Dodgson (1832–1898), more commonly known as Lewis Carroll, since seven when she first read *Alice in Wonderland*. Confused by widely varying depictions of the Victorian era author, she turned to primary sources, including newly found financial records, seeking to reconcile the contradictions. In a series of 10 essays that marry facts with Dodgson's own writings, she examines different aspects of the mysterious man's life.

Essential Profiles

Small is beautiful, especially in books. Busy people like books that give them the essential story without involving them for days or weeks at a time. Luckily for them, there are entire series of well-regarded short biographies available, including Penguin Lives, American Presidents, English Monarchs, Eminent Lives, Great Generals, and Lives and Legacies. All of these compact biographies are written by eminent authors with particular viewpoints to offer. Here are just a few of many such books.

Davis, Donald

Stonewall Jackson. **Great Generals Series**. 2007. Palgrave Macmillan. 204p. ISBN 8671403974778.

The story of Confederate General Thomas "Stonewall" Jackson (1824–1863) has many elements common to heroic legends. First, he was an orphan who proved himself as brave as his noteworthy ancestors. Then, in battle, he defeated larger and better-armed forces, risking his own life by leading attacks and commanding the respect and loyalty of his men. Ironically, his life ended soon after he was mistakenly shot by one of his own soldiers. In this compact biography, military historian Donald Davis depicts Jackson as the key general whose loss meant the Confederate Army would lose the war.

Gaunt, Peter

Oliver Cromwell. **British Library Historic Lives Series**. 2004. New York University Press. 144p. ISBN 0814731643.

This much is clear—British statesman Oliver Cromwell (1599–1658) led Puritans tired of monarchical excesses to victory in the English Civil War of 1642–1646. He then imposed many unwanted laws on an ungrateful country. Whether he was a hero with a just cause or a tyrant consolidating power to impose his own moral code is still hotly debated by historians. In this attractive compact volume in the British Library Historic Lives Series, scholar Peter Gaunt lays out the historical evidence in favor and against England's only Lord Protector.

Leuchtenburg, William E.
 Herbert Hoover. <u>American Presidents Series</u>. 2009. Times Books. 186p. ISBN:
  9780805069587.

   When Herbert Hoover (1874–1964) was elected president in 1928, he was
one of the most admired men in America, having risen from rural poverty to
become a mining engineer, prominent businessman, and international champion of humanitarian aid. Within a year of election, the stock market crashed,
leaving millions of workers jobless and their families hungry and homeless.
Unwilling to increase the federal debt, he unsuccessfully tried to mobilize the
private sector to assist the needy. In this short biography from the American
Presidents Series, historian William E. Leuchtenburg portrays Hoover as a
well-intentioned leader whose one great failure overshadowed his venerable
record of service to his country.

Mundy, Liza
 Michelle: A Biography. 2008. Simon & Schuster. 217p. ISBN 9781416599432.

   Born on the south side of Chicago just days before President Lyndon
Johnson signed the Civil Rights Act, Michelle Obama (1964–) has become
a symbol of racial equality. Aided by affirmative action to attend a magnet
school and an Ivy League college, she graduated from Harvard to become first
a corporate lawyer and then a director for nonprofit organizations. According
to *Washington Post* staff writer Liza Mundy, marriage, motherhood, and conservative pundits have not slowed Obama's rise. Writing before the 2008 election, Mundy describes a woman who as first lady is bound to have an impact
on American public policy.

Pease, Donald E.
 Theodor Seuss Geisel. <u>Lives and Legacies Series</u>. 2010. Oxford University
  Press. 178p. ISBN 9780195323023. ✑

   Theodor Seuss Geisel (1904–1991) was a successful cartoonist and illus-
trator traveling on a luxury liner in stormy seas trying to stave off a panic attack when he conceived of his first children's book, *And to Think That I Saw
It on Mulberry Street*. By the time he wrote *Oh, the Places You'll Go!*, he was
a world famous children's author revered by parents and many liberal causes.
How the Dartmouth University graduate who once drew racist cartoons for
war propaganda became a beloved cultural icon is the subject of this nicely
illustrated short biography.

Smiley, Jane
 ▶ *Charles Dickens*. <u>Penguin Lives Series</u>. 2002. Lipper/Viking. 212p. ISBN
  0670030775.

   Like many of us, novelist Charles Dickens (1812–1870) never lived up
to the ideals he professed. Although his wildly popular books urged many
reforms to improve the lives of common English people, he quietly neglected
his children and his wife while conducting secret love affairs. In this literary

biography, novelist Jane Smiley gently reconsiders the life and writings of a troubled man who moved many readers with his compassionate stories of orphans and their benefactors.

Thomson, David

Bette Davis. **Great Stars Series**. 2010. Faber and Faber. 128p. ISBN 9780865479319.

Her father said that she would be a better secretary than actress, but Bette Davis (1908–1989) wanted badly to star in movies. Her early directors doubted her public appeal, but in her prime she had more Academy Award nominations than Garbo, Hepburn, Crawford, and other actresses considered more glamorous than Davis. She excelled at playing an angry woman and with age became even more menacing. David Thomson praises Davis's talent and determination in this compact tribute to a Hollywood star.

Wallach, Jennifer Jensen

Richard Wright: From Black Boy to World Citizen. **Library of African-American Biography**. 2010. Ivan R. Dee. 197p. ISBN 9781566638241.

Born in a sharecropper's cabin in Mississippi, Richard Wright (1908–1960) was buried alongside Jean Baptiste Molière and Oscar Wilde in Paris. With only an eighth-grade education, the African American novelist moved north to Chicago and then to New York, where he wrote the highly acclaimed novel *Native Son* and a memoir *Black Boy*. The price of success, however, was high for Wright, who never felt comfortable as a spokesperson for his race. In this title from the Library of African-American Biography series, historian Jennifer Jensen Wallach recounts the unsettled life of a solitary man looking for his place in the literary world.

Epic Tales

While short biographies satisfy some readers, others welcome thick volumes that recount fully the lives of eminent people, such as world leaders, prominent artists, and legendary sports figures. These readers enjoy spending weeks with books, immersing themselves in numerous episodes of great people's lives. Biographers, who are often scholars specializing in their subjects, happily offer long biographies for which they win acclaim and loyal readers. Here are nine epic biographies for dedicated readers.

Chernow, Ron

Alexander Hamilton. 2004. Penguin Press. 818p. ISBN 1594200092. ☙

Along with James Madison, Alexander Hamilton (1757–1804) was one of the most accomplished yet least appreciated American Founding Fathers. After serving at a very young age as General George Washington's aide and advisor during the American Revolution, he led the debate over the formation of a strong constitutional government and held several important posts in the early republic. In this detailed account, historian Ron Chernow tells how the first U.S. secretary of the treasury enduringly shaped the government and the economy before the tragic duel with Aaron Burr that ended his life.

Crouch, Tom D.
The Bishop's Boys: A Life of Wilbur and Orville Wright. 1989. W. W. Norton. 606p. ISBN 0393026604.

Bachelor brothers Wilbur Wright (1867–1912) and Orville Wright (1871–1948) were the youngest sons of controversial and uncompromising clergyman Milton Wright. Never venturing far from their father's doctrine, they kept family ways—wearing ties to work (even when flying airplanes on the beach!), defending their business interests tenaciously, and always returning to the family home in Ohio. Inventing the first airplane to sustain flight is only one part of Tom D. Crouch's epic story of two American icons.

Eyman, Scott
Empire of Dreams: The Epic Life of Cecil B. DeMille. 2010. Simon & Schuster. 579p. ISBN 9780743289559.

Nothing is more fitting than an epic-sized biography of the maker of colossal movies, Cecil B. DeMille (1881–1959). The son of a playwright who had studied theology, the future director of *The Ten Commandments* began his entertainment career as an actor but was soon directing early silent films. Credited for finding many of his industry's early stars, he later supported Senator Joseph McCarthy's campaign to rid Hollywood of left-leaning actors and writers in the 1950s. In this frank but sympathetic biography, Scott Eyman recounts the life of a demanding director who always pleased the public more than the critics.

Frank, Joseph
Dostoevsky: A Writer in His Time. 2010. Princeton University Press. 959p. ISBN 9780691128191.

Early in his career, rivals called novelist Feodor Mikhailovich Dostoevsky (1821–1881) a "pimple on the face of Russian literature," claiming that he was melodramatic and too impressed by aristocracy. By the time he had written *The Brother Karamozov*, however, he was acclaimed as the voice of Russia for writing honestly about its classes and capturing the tenor of his time. In condensing his five-volume biography of Dostoevsky into one large book, award-winning author Joseph Frank recounts the career of a literary master in the context of turbulent Russian history.

Hirsch, James S.
Willie Mays: The Life, the Legend. 2010. Scribner. 628p. ISBN 9781416547907.

As a rookie outfielder for the New York Giants, Willie Mays (1931–) once caught both a fly ball and the cap that had blown from his head in a single motion. Such was the grace and talent of a man considered among baseball's greatest players and who retired second on the all-time career home runs list. In this monumental authorized biography, James S. Hirsch examines minutely the youth and professional career of a proud man who quietly advanced the cause of racial equality while entertaining the nation.

Kershaw, Ian
Hitler: 1936–1945: Nemesis. 2000. W. W. Norton. 1115p. ISBN 0393049949.

One of the biggest questions about the 20th century is how Adolf Hitler was able to convince the German people to support his radical agenda of suppression of the Jews and aggression against neighboring countries. According to historian Ian Kershaw, as president and chancellor of Germany, Hitler constantly pushed this agenda a little further with each initiative, making each seem reasonable based upon his previous requests. In this investigative biography, Kershaw lays out Hitler's last 10 years as a supreme German leader in great detail. Serious history readers who relish epic stories will enjoy this important work.

Lee, Hermione
Edith Wharton. 2007. Alfred A. Knopf. 869p. ISBN 9780375400049.

According to literary biographer Hermione Lee, novelist Edith Wharton (1862–1937) has been unfairly characterized as a snobbish high society woman. Although Wharton was born into a culture of wealth and maintained friendships with artists, intellectuals, and other people of privilege throughout her long life, she was a modern thinker who supported many causes through volunteer work and her writings. In this epic biography, Lee chronicles Wharton's difficult transformation from debutante to woman of substance.

McCullough, David
▶ *John Adams*. 2001. Simon & Schuster. 751p. ISBN 0684813637. ☙

Though revolutionary statesman John Adams (1735–1826) is considered a giant among the American Founding Fathers today, his career and reputation were often endangered in his own time. More concerned with truth and vision than with compromise, he frequently clashed with Virginia's Thomas Jefferson, New York's Alexander Hamilton, and his own Massachusetts colleagues. Drawing from Adams's own papers, renowned biographer David McCullough intimately recounts the life of a public man whose steady private life and secure marriage was his source of strength and inspiration.

Spurling, Hilary
Matisse the Master: A Life of Henri Matisse: The Conquest of Color, 1909–1954. 2005. Alfred A. Knopf. 512p. ISBN 0679434291. ☙

Rumors that he had exploited his models and collaborated with the Nazis during their occupation of France upset artist Henri Matisse (1869–1954). None of this was true, according to critic Hilary Spurling, who was granted unrestricted access to the artist's papers. In this second volume of her epic biography on

Matisse, she portrays him as a very private man, injured by the scorn of art critics. Only his ability to lose himself in his pursuit of color kept him from despair.

Investigative Reports

Biographers often briefly tell about their research in short prefaces or introductions, which may also be used to acknowledge people who have helped them research, write, and publish their books. Main biographical texts are free of references to the authors and their efforts to get their stories, but there are exceptions. Sometimes, even the author's traveling to historic sites, interviewing contemporaries, or witnessing of events is itself the stuff of good storytelling. In the following biographies, the authors use their investigative journeys as subplots to advance their stories.

Blackburn, Julia

The Emperor's Last Island: A Journey to St. Helena. 1991. Pantheon Books. 277p. ISBN 067941150X.

Lives as large as that of Napoleon Bonaparte (1769–1821) are often best studied in parts. Wanting to understand how the emperor who tried to conquer a continent endured confinement to a small volcanic island off the Atlantic coast of Africa, author Julia Blackburn read historical documents and the deposed French emperor's journals. Then, she traveled to remote St. Helena, where she visited the derelict cottage where Napoleon lived his final days. Writing sympathetically about Napoleon's imprisonment, Blackburn makes the former emperor a more human and tragic figure.

Dohrmann, George

Play Their Hearts Out: A Coach, His Star Recruit, and the Youth Basketball Machine. 2010. Ballantine Books. 422p. ISBN 9780345508607.

Though already wearing a size 14 shoe, Demetrius Walker (1991–) was only 10 when basketball coach Joe Keller recruited the youth for his talented Amateur Athletic Union (AAU) team. While Walker wanted to get free shoes, play basketball, and eventually earn a scholarship, the coach eyed sponsorships, self-promotion, and revenge against a coach who stole his previous star. In this dark dual biography, *Sports Illustrated* journalist George Dohrmann recounts from the sidelines how an AAU coach relentlessly demanded more than a boy could deliver.

Helm, Sarah

A Life in Secrets: Vera Atkins and the Missing Agents of WWII. 2005. Nan A. Talese. 493p. ISBN 038550845x. ☙

Was master spy Vera Atkins (1908–2000) the inspiration for Miss Moneypenny in Ian Fleming's James Bond novels? She would not say, but using declassified documents and Atkins family papers, journalist Sarah Helm discovered that London-based Atkins directed the movements of more than 400 spies during World War II. Unfortunately, more than 100 of them disappeared. Feeling responsible for her agents, Atkins then personally sought them or their remains after the war. With admiration, Helm recounts Atkins's secretive life.

Huang, Yunte
Charlie Chan: The Untold Story of the Honorable Detective and His Rendezvous with American History. 2010. W. W. Norton. 354p. ISBN 9780393069624.

In translations from real life to books, then to movies, characters sometimes become almost unrecognizable. Such was the case in the development of the racially stereotyped icon of Chinese detective Charlie Chan. Behind the now politically incorrect image of Chan is the forgotten story of Chang Apana (1871–1933), a respected Hawaiian policeman of Chinese descent who fought gamblers and drug sellers in Honolulu. Yunte Huang, an English professor from China, recounts his search for the real man as well as why the fictional Chan was both so popular and reviled.

Meier, Andrew
▶ *The Lost Spy: An American in Stalin's Secret Service*. 2008. W. W. Norton. 402p. ISBN 9780393060973.

In 1992, when Russian president Boris Yeltsin presented diplomat Malcolm Toon with a thin dossier about the death of Isaiah Oggins (1898–1947), it was the first news about the American who turned into a Soviet spy since his arrest in Moscow in 1939. Learning about the expatriate in 2000, *Time*'s Moscow correspondent Andrew Meier began an eight-year search for documents about Oggins in the newly opened KGB archives. In this investigative biography, Meier reveals why the idealistic Oggins was murdered on the direct order of Soviet premier Joseph Stalin.

Sheehan, Neil
A Fiery Peace in a Cold War: Bernard Schriever and the Ultimate Weapon. 2009. Random House. 534p. ISBN 9780679422846.

Air Force Major General Bernard Schriever (1910–2005) believed that assuring mutual annihilation was the best strategy against the use of atomic weapons. Even among the proponents of the military-industrial complex, that was not an easy sell in the 1950s. In a biography taking Schriever from his days as a young immigrant to his retirement, award-winning journalist Neil Sheehan recounts how the general defended his Intercontinental Ballistic Missile Program against the opposition of powerful foes in the military and Congress.

Thomas, Gordon, and Martin Dillon
Robert Maxwell, Israel's Superspy: The Life and Murder of a Media Mogul. 2002. Carroll and Graf. 448p. ISBN 0786710780.

Robert Maxwell (1923–1991) was a fabulously wealthy publisher of British newspapers. Because he was a personal friend of Prime Minister Margaret

Thatcher and Soviet president Mikhail Gorbachev, he was privy to many sensitive conversations of strategic importance. Who would have suspected that he was also secretly employed by Israel's spy service Mossad? In this thrilling investigative biography, authors Gordon Thomas and Martin Dillon reveal that Maxwell's disappearance at sea was not an accident.

Vincent, Isabel
Gilded Lily: Lily Safra: The Making of One of the World's Wealthiest Widows. 2010. HarperCollins. 324p. ISBN 9780061133930.

Wolf White Watkins, a British rail engineer living in Argentina, insisted that his daughter marry money. Being his obedient daughter, Lily Safra (1934–) has done so four times and become one of the world's wealthiest women. Two husbands died suspiciously, fueling rumors that Safra is both greedy and murderous. Using court records, news reports, and interviews, veteran investigative reporter Isabel Vincent lets readers decide whether the widow known for funding philanthropic causes while living an opulent life deserves sympathy or condemnation.

Friendly Memories

Biographers often interview people who knew their subjects, seeking stories and opinions to enrich their narratives. Sometimes, these coworkers, friends, or family members feel compelled to write their own books, which tend to be sympathetic accounts even when they admit the subject's faults. The following are eight biographies written by friendly authors who remain focused on their subjects and not themselves, keeping the accounts from being memoirs.

Cole, K. C.
Something Incredibly Wonderful Happens: Frank Oppenheimer and the World He Made Up. 2009. Houghton Mifflin Harcourt. 396p. ISBN 9780151008223.

The odds of a physicist blacklisted in 1949 for communist sympathies ever returning to his profession were poor. Unable to find work in his field, Frank Oppenheimer (1912–1985) turned to cattle ranching in rural Colorado to support his family. The retreat turned into a golden opportunity as he discovered that he loved teaching when he helped local students with state science fair competitions. Friend and science journalist K.C. Cole tells how by creating the Exploratorium, an innovative teaching museum in San Francisco, the rejuvenated Oppenheimer led a revolution in science education.

Finch, Christopher
Chuck Close: Life. 2010. Prestel. 350p. ISBN 9783791336770.

Art curator Christopher Finch has known contemporary artist Chuck Close (1940–), famous for his larger-than-life portraits, for more than 40 years. The two are part of the New York art scene and often discuss the ever-changing world of art. Finch's wife Linda even sat for a Close painting, now in the Akron Museum of Art. With much affection and respect, Finch tells a very personal story about how Close overcame learning disabilities in childhood and later a debilitating heart attack to become one of the most recognized American artists since Andy Warhol.

Fisher, June Breton

When Money Was in Fashion: Henry Goldman, Goldman Sachs, and the Founding of Wall Street. 2010. Palgrave Macmillan. 278p. ISBN 9780230617506.

Author June Breton Fisher remembers her grandfather, investment banker Henry Goldman (1854–1937), son of Goldman Sachs founder Marcus Goldman, for his warmth and his interesting friends, including scientists Albert Einstein and Max Born. Naturally, she objects to how he has been written out of corporate histories of Sears Roebuck and Woolworths for vocally supporting Germany during World War I. She argues that neither company would have been as profitable without his leadership. Mixing family history with insider stories of the struggles within Goldman Sachs, she portrays Goldman as a man of strict business principle and compassion for philanthropic causes.

Hoppes, Jonna Doolittle

Calculated Risk: The Extraordinary Life of Jimmy Doolittle—Aviation Pioneer and World War II Hero. 2005. Santa Monica Press. 334p. ISBN 1891661442.

Known to author Jonna Doolittle Hoppes as Grandpa, pioneering pilot Jimmy Doolittle (1896–1993) drew both praise and criticism during his long career, much of it spent with the U.S. armed forces. In that time, he set speed records for transcontinental flights, trained many fighter pilots, and led bombing missions over Japan and Germany. In this photo-filled biography with family stories, Hoppes describes Doolittle's courage and love for flying.

House, Adrian

The Great Safari: The Lives of George and Joy Adamson, Famous for Born Free. 1993. William Morrow. 465p. ISBN 0688101410. ☙

Viewers of the hit movie *Born Free*, based on the book by Joy Adamson (1910–1980), saw Joy and her husband George Adamson (1906–1989) as a devoted couple brought together by their love of big cats and the East African landscape. In the wake of *Born Free*, they published numerous other books about their lions, leopards, and cheetahs. After both were shockingly murdered nine years apart, their editor Adrian House was left with only their copious journals with which to tell the true story of their troubled marriage. With much candor, he fulfilled their wishes with this heartbreaking book.

Klein, Edward

Farewell, Jackie. 2004. Viking. 212p. ISBN 0670033316.

Though prolific Kennedy biographer Edward Klein was not a member of Jacqueline Kennedy Onassis's (1929–1994) inner circle, he was close enough to dine with her regularly and visit her home. When she learned that she had cancer, he was among the people she told. While inserting some short flashbacks to key moments in the former first lady's life, Klein tenderly chronicles her last brave months with friends and family.

Kogan, Rick
▶ *America's Mom: The Life, Lessons, and Legacy of Ann Landers*. 2003. William Morrow. 260p. ISBN 0060544783.

Rick Kogan was a family friend and the final editor for advice columnist Ann Landers (1918–2002). After her death, he visited an auction of her belongings where he met collectors who hoped to catch a glimpse of her life in her possessions. Kogan uses items from the auction to introduce various phases of her long and sometimes glorious life. The story of her estrangement and reconciliation with her equally famous twin sister Abigail Van Buren, rival advice columnist, is included.

Roberts, David
The Last of His Kind: The Life and Adventures of Bradford Washburn, America's Boldest Mountaineer. 2009. William Morrow. 334p. ISBN 9780061560941.

When 24-year-old Brad Washburn (1910–2007) led a 3-month hiking and climbing expedition across Alaska in 1934, vast areas of the territory's interior filled with mountains and glacial rivers were unmapped. Without outside communications, he and his companions could have simply disappeared. In this tribute to his mentor, climber David Roberts recounts the many dangers faced by the intrepid Washburn, a noted mountain photographer, cartographer, and first man to climb nine difficult American peaks.

Quoted Lives

Many biographies include quotations from their subjects. Short statements may be woven into the texts, and passages from speeches, letters, or published writings may be inserted with increased margins to identify them to readers. In some cases, the quotations are so numerous, the books border on being constructed memoirs. Here are seven biographies in which the authors let their subjects tell much of their own stories.

Minutaglio, Bill, and W. Michael Smith
Molly Ivins: A Rebel Life. 2009. Public Affairs. 335p. ISBN 9781586487171.

Although she was groomed to be a Houston debutante, journalist Molly Ivins (1944–2007) found her calling in smoky pressrooms and marble halls of government from which she told comic stories of bumbling and corrupt politicians. Her sarcastic wit and uncompromising honesty lost her several plum jobs, but she always found another magazine or newspaper eager to print her stories. By the time of her death, she was a widely read columnist and a best-selling author. Journalists Bill Minutaglio and W. Michael Smith toast their missing comrade in this quote-filled tribute.

Rogak, Lisa
Haunted Heart: The Life and Times of Stephen King. 2009. Thomas Dunne Books. 310p. ISBN 9780312377328.

Novelist Stephen King (1947–) lied when he told reporters that he rests from writing on Christmas and his birthday to seem more normal. The obsessive author writes every day to cope with his many fears—the dark, spiders, deformity, inability to write, and especially the number 13. In this account filled with quotes from 40 years of King's interviews, pop literature biographer Lisa Rogak shows that, despite his claims to being a boring subject, King's messy and neurotic life is a compelling story.

Rubin Stuart, Nancy
Muse of the Revolution: The Secret Pen of Mercy Otis Warren and the Founding of a Nation. 2008. Beacon Press. 314p. ISBN 9780807055168. ☙

Mercy Otis Warren (1728–1814) was a friend of Abigail Adams and Martha Washington, wife of a prominent Plymouth patriot, prolific letter writer, anonymous author of satirical poems and plays during the early days of the American Revolution, and one of the country's first historians. Biographer Nancy Rubin Stuart incorporates letters to and from Warren in this detailed account of how an educated woman dealt with motherhood, war, prejudice, and the desire to be a full participant in her society.

Seal, Mark
▶ *Wildflower: An Extraordinary Life and Untimely Death in Africa*. 2009. Random House. 232p. ISBN 9781400067367.

In this heart-wrenching biography, Mark Seal recounts the life of wildlife photographer Joan Root (1936–2006), setting her failed marriage to cinematographer Alan Root and her tragic murder against the stunning scenery of Africa's Great Rift Valley. Using Root's letters to her mother and friends, the author offers readers an intimate look at a woman who was very loyal to an unworthy husband. *Wildflower* is a riveting story with elements of adventure, romance, and crime.

Spring, Justin
Secret Historian: The Life and Times of Samuel Steward, Professor, Tattoo Artist, and Sexual Renegade. 2010. Farrar, Straus and Giroux. 478p. ISBN 9780374281342.

The life of homosexuals during the middle decades of the 20th century is poorly documented, as gays hid in fear of being arrested for breaking strict antisodomy laws. Forgotten novelist and poet Samuel Steward (1909–1993), however, kept daily journals and a card file detailing his sexual encounters, which biographer Justin Spring discovered. Quoting from Steward's own writings, Spring recounts the novelist's life and friendships with singer Rudolph Valentino, author Gertrude Stein, sex researcher Alfred Kinsey, and many anonymous men.

Unger, Harlow Giles
Lion of Liberty: Patrick Henry and the Call to a New Nation. 2010. Da Capo Press. 322p. ISBN 9780306818868.

As courtroom lawyer and governor of Virginia, Patrick Henry (1736–1799) was known for his eloquent speeches. In crying "give me liberty or give me death" at the Second Revolutionary Convention of Virginia in 1775, he was the first of the Founding Fathers to call for independence. It is fitting that historian Harlow Giles Unger fills his admiring biography of Henry with the statesman's own words.

Wills, Garry
Saint Augustine. 1999. Viking. 152p. ISBN 0670886106.

It is by words and not deeds that Saint Augustine (354–430) is known, according to award-winning author Garry Wills. Though he was just a bishop of little authority in Hippo, a Roman outpost on the coast of Africa, Augustine wrote profusely, often dictating late into the night. After 16 centuries, not all of what he said about himself is well understood. Using many quotes and applying modern scholarship, Wills corrects many of the myths about Augustine's sinful youth and theological thought.

Words and Pictures

If you accept the adage "a picture is worth a thousand words," then a series of pictures may be strung together to tell a good story. This has proved true in biography. Photobiographies have proved especially popular to celebrate the careers of celebrities and world leaders. Even famous scientists, such as Alexander Graham Bell and Albert Einstein, make good subjects for highly illustrated biographies. Here are nine good examples.

Bond, Jennie
Elizabeth: Fifty Glorious Years. 2002. Reader's Digest. 160p. ISBN 0762103698.

Being first a princess and then queen, Elizabeth II has been in front of a camera all her life. For the 50th anniversary of Elizabeth's reign, author Jennie Bond wrote an admiring profile of the queen for a large collection of royal photographs. The photos tell a story of a woman who goes wherever she is asked, inspecting mines, launching ships, attending weddings, and meeting world leaders. Whether in her crown, a colorful hat, or in a scarf, Elizabeth is rarely alone and often smiling. Readers who follow the British Royal Family will enjoy this book.

Cohen, David Elliot
Nelson Mandela: A Life in Photographs. 2009. Sterling. 221p. ISBN 9781402777073. ☙

Nelson Mandela (1918–) has been one of the most charismatic figures of the past century. Already photogenic and well-spoken, he drew the attention of cameramen even in the early days of the African National Congress when he served as one of its leaders. His imprisonment stopped the flow of images until his dramatic release in 1990. The texts of his most famous speeches are included with many historical photographs in this inspiring biography.

Cross, Charles R.
Cobain Unseen. 2008. Little Brown. 159p. ISBN 9780316033725.

A museum could be filled with the debris of rock musician Kurt Cobain's life (1967–1994). In addition to his quirky paintings, drawings, and photographs, it could display his diverse collections—everything from old toys to heart-shaped boxes. Many of these items seem incongruous with the life of the drug-addicted rock star who lived in a series of cheap apartments before buying a 15-room mansion. In this visual biography with fold-out pages and pictures in pockets, rock music journalist Charles R. Cross portrays Cobain as an intense seeker who never found what he sought.

Gillespie, Marcia, Rosa Johnson Butler, and Richard A. Long
Maya Angelou: A Glorious Celebration. 2008. Doubleday. 191p. ISBN 9780385511087.

Poet and essayist Maya Angelou (1928–) has already told her life very well in a series of memoirs, starting with *I Know Why the Caged Bird Sings*. Because her fans still want to know more, two of her best friends and a niece have collected photographs and documents highlighting Angelou's long career as not only a writer but also a dancer, singer, and actor. Text and photos showing her with friends James Baldwin, Malcolm X, and Oprah Winfrey support the idea that Angelou is a central figure of African American culture.

Grosvenor, Edwin S., and Morgan Wesson
Alexander Graham Bell: The Life and Times of the Man Who Invented the Telephone. 1997. Harry Abrams. 304p. ISBN 0810940051.

Most modern readers know Alexander Graham Bell (1847–1922) only as the inventor of the telephone. Few know that he also invented a phonograph, a respirator, a metal detector, and early airplane parts. In addition, he also experimented in deaf education, supported Montessori schools, and was a key founder of the National Geographic Society. Despite the narrow implication of this photo book's subtitle, authors Edwin S. Grosvenor and Morgan Wesson show Bell as a respected public man who transformed industry and improved the quality of life in American homes.

Isaacson, Walter
Einstein: The Life of a Genius. 2009. HarperCollins. 94p. ISBN 9780061893896.

With his thick moustache and unkempt hair, Albert Einstein (1879–1955) was an instantly recognizable figure who was photographed frequently throughout his life. In this photo album, biographer Walter Isaacson combines images of Einstein with those of the physicist's family and colleagues and with important document facsimiles, such as a report card from the Aarau School, handwritten lecture notes, and his letter to President Franklin D. Roosevelt about the possible construction of atomic bombs. This combination of short texts and historical images helps readers understand Einstein in his time.

Souza, Pete
The Rise of Barack Obama. 2008. Triumph Books. 160p. ISBN 9781600781636.

Photobiographies of successful politicians, especially U.S. presidents, have been a staple of publishing for years. In 2005, Pete Souza, former official photographer of the Reagan White House, recognized the potential of Barack Obama and won an assignment to follow the junior senator from Illinois around the Capitol and on dramatic visits abroad. In black-and-white photographs that have a 1960s Civil Rights Era tone, Souza documents the quick rise of a charismatic young leader.

Verlhac, Pierre-Henri, and Yann-Brice Dherbier, eds.
Paul Newman: A Life in Pictures. 2006. Chronicle Books. 205p. ISBN 9780811857260.

Having said "A man can only be judged by his actions, and not by his good intentions or his beliefs," a big photo book of actor Paul Newman (1925–2008) at work and play seems an appropriate biography. Looking through its well-chosen publicity shots, news photos, and candid family snapshots, readers will discover a confident man who played many roles. The photobiography works well as both an introduction and a tribute to Newman's career.

Wertheimer, Alfred
▶ *Elvis 1956*. 2009. Welcome Books. 127p. ISBN 9781599620732.

When RCA Records hired Alfred Wertheimer to photograph their newly signed recording star Elvis Presley (1935–1977) performing on the *Dorsey Brothers' Stage Show*, the photographer had never heard of the 21-year-old singer. Wertheimer quickly recognized Presley as a great photographic subject. Within four months, he shot hundreds of candid photos of the young Presley on stage, backstage, in hotels, on the street, on trains, and at home. In this combination photo and essay book, Wertheimer reveals Presley as a cool entertainer prepared for his fame.

Chapter Five

Mood

We're often in the mood for books of love, adventure, mystery, and inspiration, and they do not have to be genre fiction. Biographies express as great a range of moods as their fictional counterparts and can satisfy many readers' longing for emotional atmosphere. Furthermore, they may merit more thought and discussion than their fictional kin for affirming that love, adventure, and other highly sought experiences truly exist.

Books in this chapter support the old saying "truth is stranger than fiction." Few novelists would create a character as urban and pleasant as E. B. White or one as tragically unfortunate as Mary Todd Lincoln. World War I pilot and race car driver Eddie Rickenbacker's life was more adventurous than the heroes in many dime-store novels. Twelfth-century-philosopher Peter Abelard (1079–1142) and his Parisian student Heloise set a standard for literary romance that has rarely been met. Are there fictional characters as strange as pianists Glenn Gould or Liberace?

In this chapter are eight book lists featuring biographies of particular moods that are used across the literatures of fiction and nonfiction alike. "Denial of Danger," "Celebration of Romance," and "Engaging Enigmas" share many of the same appeal factors as adventure, romance, and mystery novels. "Torment of Tragedy" taps a current found across both genre and literary fiction, and "Heartwarming Stories" will appeal to fans of gentle reads. The appeals of "Psychological Depths," "Pure Nostalgia," and "Glorious Gossip" inhabit various forms of nonfiction and periodical literature that constantly draw readers.

Denial of Danger

Climbing unconquered mountains, rafting untamed rivers, and flying experimental aircraft are all risky deeds that define some people as adventurers. Imagine how exciting it would be to join them. Sometimes, it is thrilling just to read about the feats of fearless people, such as World War I pilot Eddie Rickenbacker or Grand Canyon explorer John Wesley Powell. The following biographies recount true adventures that will satisfy readers craving daring in the face of danger.

Gentile, Olivia

Life List: A Woman's Quest for the World's Most Amazing Birds. 2009. Bloomsbury. 345p. ISBN 9781596911697.

Phoebe Snetsinger (1931–1999) would ride a horse for 10 hours over rocky terrain in the rain to see a rare bird. She would even skirt through war-torn Zaire and sneak into the ruins of Rwanda to add to her life list. She also missed her mother's funeral, her daughter's wedding, and her husband's magic shows while becoming the first person to ever see 8,000 of the earth's approximately 9,700 recognized bird species. Journalist Olivia Gentile takes readers to the world's most remote locations in this intimate look at a frustrated housewife turned international adventurer.

Gillman, Peter, and Leni Gillman

The Wildest Dream: The Biography of George Mallory. 2000. Mountaineers Books. 288p. ISBN 089886741X.

The peak of Mount Everest in Tibet had not been reached by westerners when climber George Mallory (1886–1924) made his third attempt. He disappeared up the mountain and his remains were not found until 1999. Did he reach the top? What drove a teacher to leave his young family repeatedly to attempt such a dangerous climb? Using interviews and family papers, authors Peter Gillman and Leni Gillman revisit the obsessive and ill-fated life of an early 20th-century mountaineer.

Jeffers, H. Paul

▶ *Ace of Aces: The Life of Capt. Eddie Rickenbacker*. 2003. Presidio Press. 343p. ISBN 0891417915.

Born in a time of dime-novel heroes, pilot and race car driver Eddie Rickenbacker (1890–1973) led as exciting a life as any boy from Ohio could imagine. The highly decorated World War I flying ace barnstormed across America in early planes, founded Eastern Airlines, drove the Indianapolis Speedway, and met presidents and movie stars. After re-enlisting in World War II, he was lost at sea for 24 days. In this action-packed biography, H. Paul Jeffers recounts a long life filled with adventure.

Niven, Jennifer
Ada Blackjack: A True Story of Survival in the Arctic. 2003. Hyperion. 431p. ISBN 0786868635.

 After being abandoned by her husband in Nome, Alaska, in 1921, Inuit seamstress Ada Blackjack (1898–1983) put her son into an orphanage and joined an expedition to Wrangle Island, an isolated dot in the Arctic Ocean, north of Siberia. The organizer of the mission was the controversial Canadian explorer Vilhjalmar Stefansson, whose previous ventures had ended in disaster. Two years later, newspapers proclaimed Blackjack, the only member of the expedition to be rescued, a modern Robinson Crusoe. Using diaries, letters, and interviews, Jennifer Niven looks back at the life of a tough young woman who tasted fame before receding back into poverty.

O'Brien, Michael
Mrs. Adams in Winter: A Journey in the Last Days of Napoleon. 2010. Farrar Straus and Giroux. 364p. ISBN 9780374215811. ☙

 As the wife of an American diplomat in early 19th-century Europe, Louisa Catherine Adams (1775–1852) was not expected to have adventures. Her role was to assist her husband John Quincy Adams by entertaining dignitaries, a task made difficult by his haughty idealism. Left behind in St. Petersburg, Russia, when John was made ambassador to France in 1815, Louisa took a risky journey with her young son through war-torn Europe to join her husband in Paris. In describing her remarkable passage, historian Michael O'Brien portrays Adams as a woman with the strength to tactfully stand up to border guards, innkeepers, bureaucrats, and, ultimately, her own husband.

Soskice, Janet
The Sisters of the Sinai: How Two Lady Adventurers Discovered the Hidden Gospels. 2009. Alfred A. Knopf. 316p. ISBN 9781400041336.

 When wealthy Scottish lawyer John Smith died in 1866, his 19-year-old twin daughters surprised their neighbors by wasting no time in mourning. Instead, they spent part of their large inheritance to tour Egypt. The adventure proved to be just a prelude to the later travels of Agnes Smith Lewis (1843–1926) and Margaret Dunlap Gibson (1843–1920), scholarly sisters who spoke numerous modern and ancient languages. Theologian Janet Soskice tells a lively tale of women who in middle age ventured to remote monasteries of the Sinai to find ancient Bible manuscripts.

Winters, Kathleen C.
Anne Morrow Lindbergh: First Lady of the Air. 2006. Palgrave Macmillan. 241p. ISBN 9781403969323.

 Remembered for her best-selling memoirs and for being the wife of pioneering pilot Charles Lindbergh, Anne Morrow Lindbergh (1906–2001) was also an accomplished pilot who partnered with Charles on many exploratory flights for Pan American Airlines. For a decade, she flew over vast oceans and remote continents, testing routes for commercial flights; when not at the controls, she operated delicate radio equipment. Using Lindbergh's papers, author and pilot Kathleen C. Winters recounts a challenging and emotional period in the brave woman's life.

Worster, Donald
A River Running West: The Life of John Wesley Powell. 2001. Oxford University Press. 673p. ISBN 0195099915.

Although he lost an arm in the battle at Shiloh in the American Civil War, John Wesley Powell (1834–1902) was determined to study the geology of the unexplored West. He led a geologic exploration of the uncharted Colorado River and Grand Canyon, a dangerous adventure that featured scientific discovery, scarce supplies, and mutiny. Donald Worster chronicles the evolution of a conservationist who overcame his handicaps and inspired the American parks movement.

Celebration of Romance

Romance fiction is frequently reported to be the top-selling segment of the American book market. Devoted readers will buy or check out from their libraries stacks of books filled with love stories. Most nonfiction does not have romantic appeal, but the following biographies featuring celebrated couples, such as medieval France's Heloise and Abelard and Hollywood's Bogart and Bacall, may please readers who enjoy having their heartstrings pulled.

Andersen, Christopher
Somewhere in Heaven: The Remarkable Love Story of Dana and Christopher Reeve. 2008. Hyperion. 238p. ISBN 9781401323028.

Courage in the face of tragedy defined the marriage of singer Dana Morosini (1961–2006) to actor Christopher Reeve (1952–2004). Celebrity biographer Christopher Andersen reports that it was love at first sight for the athletic couple, then five years of cautious courting, which was followed by total devotion. They sailed boats, flew small planes, and rode horses together and with their children. Three years after their wedding, Christopher's horse-riding accident began a series of tragedies that are recounted by Andersen in this sympathetic dual biography.

Burge, James
Heloise and Abelard: A New Biography. 2003. HarperSanFrancisco. 319p. ISBN 0060736631. ⮒

Because a series of eloquent letters were written 900 years ago, the passionate and ultimately heartbreaking love affair of philosopher Peter Abelard (1079–1142) of Brittany and his Parisian student Heloise (1095–1163) is now literary legend.

When the couple's relationship was exposed, the two were forced into monastic lives to which neither was truly suited. Using the long-known letters written late in their lives with newly identified letters written during the secret affair, author James Burge reveals two people with surprisingly modern ideas about love.

Edwards, Anne
The Reagans: Portrait of a Marriage. 2003. St. Martins Press. 420p. ISBN 0312285000.

In February 1952, Ronald Reagan (1911–2004) called on Dr. Loyal Davis of Scottsdale, Arizona, to ask permission to marry his stepdaughter. It was an unusual act, for Nancy Davis (1921–) was a 30-year-old actress and Reagan was a 41-year-old divorcé. Neither needed permission, but the bride wanted family approval and Reagan agreed to her request. According to biographer Anne Edwards, the Hollywood marriage of the future president and first lady would always include such easy accommodations, even when there was trouble with children and political aides. In this book, Edwards tells Reagan family stories as though she witnessed them.

Gelles, Edith B.
▶ *Abigail and John: Portrait of a Marriage*. 2009. William Morrow. 339p. ISBN 9780061353871. ☙

John Adams (1735–1826) and Abigail Adams (1744–1818) were of necessity letter writers. Apart so frequently, with John at the Continental Congress in Philadelphia, on diplomatic missions in Europe, or in the new seat of government in New York or Washington, while she was in Massachusetts, the couple was constantly writing. Abigail told John of their home and business matters, while he reported on his work for the country. Throughout, they affectionately advised each other, never hesitating to be frank in disagreements. Adams scholar Edith B. Gelles recounts a life of letters in this intimate dual biography.

Gill, Gillian
We Two: Victoria and Albert: Rulers, Partners, Rivals. 2009. Ballantine Books. 460p. ISBN 9780345484055.

When Queen Victoria of Great Britain (1819–1901) invited her cousin Albert of Saxe-Coberg (1819–1861) to visit in 1839, she did so reluctantly. She had already dismissed numerous suitors and was certain she could rule the empire quite well without a consort. To her surprise, she liked the young man and proposed to him two days later. The headstrong queen would not, however, make him king. In this portrait of a marriage, author Gillian Gill recounts the passionate relationship of two lovers both intent on being the head of the household and the nation.

Hyams, Joe
Bogart and Bacall: A Love Story. 1975. David McKay Company. 245p. ISBN 0679505490.

He descended from a wealthy and long-established New York family, while she was the child of poor Jewish immigrants. He was 44 and she just 19.

Though their romance seemed unlikely, actors Humphrey Bogart (1899–1957) and Lauren Bacall (1924–) fell in love instantly, according to Hollywood columnist Joe Hyams. In this anecdotal dual biography, the admiring author describes the star couple's courtship and marriage.

Markus, Julia
Dared and Done: The Marriage of Elizabeth Barrett and Robert Browning. 1995. Alfred A. Knopf. 382p. ISBN 0679416021.

What could be more classically romantic than the love affair of two poets? At the time of their meeting, Elizabeth Barrett (1806–1861) was a well-known poet with fans in both England and the United States, living under the care of a domineering father. Robert Browning (1812 1889), a young admirer with a newly published volume of verse, asked to meet the invalid Barrett, who was suffering from a "derangement of some highly important organ." In this intimate dual biography, novelist Julia Markus utilizes letters to tell of a famous marriage of minds.

Schiff, Stacy
Véra (Mrs. Vladimir Nabokov). 1999. Random House. 456p. ISBN 0679447903. ☙

Véra Nabokov (1902–1991) was not the woman behind the success of novelist Vladimir Nabokov—she was right beside him. According to biographer Stacy Schiff, Véra and Vladimir were seldom apart even for a few hours during 52 years of marriage. Véra managed the appointments, publishers, travel, and other everyday affairs; she also proofed all her husband's writings. In her intimate account of a close marriage, Schiff reports that despite differing public opinions about his wife, Vladimir adored the woman to whom he dedicated every book.

Engaging Enigmas

Many of us love mysteries. While fiction has its detective stories and police procedurals, biography is not without its own mysteries seeking answers to difficult questions about historical figures. Was Anna Anderson Manahan really Russian Princess Anastasia? Why did pianist Glenn Gould retire from public performance? Was Harry Houdini a spy? The following biographies challenge readers to solve puzzles that may be as hard as or harder to solve than the mysteries faced by fictional sleuths.

Bazzana, Kevin
Wondrous Strange: The Life and Art of Glenn Gould. 2004. Oxford University Press. 528p. ISBN 0195174402.

After performing his last concert in April 1964, classical pianist Glenn Gould (1932–1982) planned to devote himself to recording master works and developing new sound equipment. He hoped to work out of the limelight, but withdrawing to his Toledo home only increased interest in his eccentricities. Thus began a life of dodging fans, reporters, and scholars, all of them wanting to know why he would not return to the concert stage. Using interviews and Gould's personal papers, Kevin Bazzana examines the strange ways of a life-long hypochondriac and recluse.

Davis, Natalie Zemon
Trickster Travels: A Sixteenth-Century Muslim between Worlds. 2006. Hill and Wang. 435p. ISBN 0809094347.

Captured by Spanish pirates in 1518, Muslim diplomat and scholar al-Hasan al-Wassan (1485?–?) was taken to Pope Leo X for questioning about Turkish plots against the pontiff. After being baptized a Christian 18 months later, al-Wassan took the name Giovan Lioni Africano and was freed to live as a scholar in Rome. When the city was sacked by Spaniards and Germans in 1527, al-Wassan disappeared. Did he escape to Morocco? Using al-Wassan's writings and notes that he wrote in Vatican Library books, historian Natalie Zemon Davis reveals a man adroit at living in many cultures.

Kalush, William, and Larry Sloman
▶ *The Secret Life of Houdini: The Making of America's First Superhero*. 2006. Atria Books. 592p. ISBN 9780743272070.

The story of magician and escape artist Harry Houdini (1874–1926) sounds like a movie plot aimed at adolescent boys. While visiting foreign countries to entertain his fans, Houdini used his spare moments and many con-tacts to spy for the U.S. Secret Service. He also used his vast knowledge of trickery to help police expose charlatans claiming to have psychic powers. According to authors William Kalush and Larry Sloman, however, Houdini's story is true. In this admiring biography, they reveal new evidence of the magi-cian's secret life.

Lovell, James Blair
Anastasia: The Lost Princess. 1991. Regnery Gateway. 512p. ISBN 0895265362.

Up to her death, Anna Anderson Manahan (?–1984) insisted that she was Princess Anastasia, the youngest daughter of Czar Nicholas II. By that time, her tale of escape from the Russian Revolution had been the inspira-tion of numerous novels, plays, and movies, but it was rejected by most historians. Author James Blair Lovell studied archived documents and inter-viewed the subject over the course of her last 12 years. In this investigative biography, he describes the life of a woman who lived the life of Cinderella in reverse.

Lycett, Andrew
The Man Who Created Sherlock Holmes: The Life and Times of Sir Arthur Conan Doyle. 2007. Free Press. 559p. ISBN 9780743275231.

Master detective Sherlock Holmes was a clear-thinking man in a con-fused time, an era when Darwin's theories of evolution challenged Victorian orthodoxy and unquestioned religious faith. While Holmes knew his mind, his creator, the physician and novelist Arthur Conan Doyle (1859–1930), struggled to unite his trust in science with his longing for spiritual assurance. Using previously unseen diaries and letters, biographer Andrew Lycett attempts to solve the mysteries of Doyle's contradictory nature.

Nicholl, Charles
Lodger Shakespeare: His Life on Silver Street. 2008. Viking. 377p. ISBN 9780670018505. ⮂

According to biographer Charles Nicholl, William Shakespeare (1564–1616) wrote the plays for which he is famous, but there are other questions to answer about his life. While at the height of his career, the playwright lived for 10 years along Silver Street in London. Combing through 400-year-old leases, bills of sale, tax records, and lawsuits, Nicholl discovered Shakespeare's name on numerous documents. Matching the famous lodger's everyday activities with words from his plays, Nicholl draws conclusions about the bard's political and religious beliefs, financial dealings, and personal relationships.

Pyron, Darden Asbury
Liberace: An American Boy. 2000. University of Chicago Press. 494p. ISBN 0226686671.

Born in Milwaukee with the Polish first name Wladziu, Liberace (1919–1987) charmed television audiences with flashy clothes, a feminine voice, silly anecdotes, and virtuoso performances of Mozart, Rachmaninoff, and Gershwin piano concertos. Viewed as a comic, most fans rejected the idea that he really was gay. In this intimate biography, cultural historian Darden Asbury Pyron reveals a religious and political conservative who never worried that his homosexuality contradicted his otherwise traditional values.

Steinmeyer, Jim
Charles Fort: The Man Who Invented the Supernatural. 2008. Jeremy P. Tarcher/Penguin. 332p. ISBN 9781585426409.

In his time and in ours, there is no agreement about the intentions of Charles Fort (1874–1932), a failed novelist who successfully published books about paranormal events, such as supernatural forces and extraterrestrial visitors to Earth. Did he truly believe the content of his controversial books? Was he seriously questioning traditional science, or was he a savvy businessman? In this quote-filled biography, historian Jim Steinmeyer submits copious evidence for the curious reader to evaluate.

Wallis, Michael
Billy the Kid: The Endless Ride. 2007. Norton. 328p. ISBN 9780393060683.

The identity of the outlaw known as Billy the Kid is not certain. He may have been Henry McCarty (1859–1881) of New York, also known as William

H. Bonney. His reasons for being in the nearly lawless New Mexico Territory and his exact role in several crimes are still unknown. Even the circumstances of his death are questioned. In this true crime biography, western historian Michael Wallis skillfully constructs from the best evidence a solution to a frontier mystery.

Torment of Tragedy

Tragedy has been a great theme in literature since the ancient Greek playwrights staged their dramas in the marble theaters that still attract tourists today, and Shakespeare penned tragic plays that are now the foundation of serious theater. Recognizing the everlasting appeal of misfortune and calamity, modern biographers take the stories of the ill-fated, such as presidential widow Mary Todd Lincoln and rock guitarist Jimi Hendrix, and craft tragic biographies that have readers crying for more.

Bego, Mark
I Fall to Pieces: The Music and the Life of Patsy Cline. 1995. Adams Publishing. 258p. ISBN 1558504761.
> Patsy Cline's life reads like a soap opera plot, full of surprising twists and shocking events. After she graduated from singing in roadside bars to Nashville shows, her first recording company cheated her, her second husband beat her, and she was nearly killed in an auto accident. While she was in the hospital recovering from the latter, her recording "I Fall to Pieces" topped the national country music charts. According to author Mark Bego, in death Cline joined Marilyn Monroe and Judy Garland as the tragic heroines of their era.

Black, Timothy
When Heart Turns Rock Solid: The Lives of Three Puerto Rican Brothers On and Off the Streets. 2009. Pantheon Books. 421p. ISBN 9780307377746.
> Many Puerto Ricans living in Springfield, Massachusetts, belong to a class that sociologist Timothy Black calls the permanently poor. Lack of jobs and educational opportunity combine with self-destructive behaviors to keep entire families down. Escape is rare. Following the lives of Julio Rivera (1972–) and his younger brothers Fausto and Sammy, the author gives readers an intimate tour of a world that affluent Americans are ignoring.

Clinton, Catherine
▶ *Mrs. Lincoln: A Life*. 2009. HarperCollins. 415p. ISBN 9780060760403. ☙
> By the time Mary Todd Lincoln (1818–1882) witnessed the assassination of her husband in 1865, she had already lost two sons to childhood illnesses and watched her family divide over the issues of Southern succession from the Union. Her life as a widow was filled with debts, betrayal, and bad press. Since her death, unsympathetic biographers have portrayed her as both manipulative and mad. How could Abraham Lincoln have been almost universally admired

and his wife so worthy of scorn? Known for her books on American women, historian Catherine Clinton carefully reexamines the life of the woman who loved and inspired a great president.

Cross, Charles R.
Room Full of Mirrors: A Biography of Jimi Hendrix. 2005. Hyperion. 384p. ISBN 1401300286.

Sometimes artistic achievement is a poor substitute for normalcy. Born into the poverty of Seattle's projects and after losing his mother at an early age, rock guitarist Jimi Hendrix sought refuge in his music. Despite his virtuosity, he never felt fulfilled. Music journalist Charles R. Cross recounts how racial prejudice, bad management, bad press, and drug addiction kept Hendrix from enjoying the acclaim of being his generation's greatest rock guitarist.

Helfer, Andrew
Malcolm X: A Graphic Biography. 2006. Hill and Wang. 102p. ISBN 9780809095049.

Even before the Great Depression, the black Nebraska family into which Malcolm Little (1925–1965) was born was desperately poor and targeted by the Ku Klux Klan, which resented his father's black separatist sermons. The family suffered more attacks after moving to Wisconsin, and his father was murdered in Michigan. Malcolm was placed in foster care and eventually landed in prison. Assisted by the dramatic drawings of Randy DuBurke, DC Comics editor Andrew Helfer recounts the troubled life and tragic death of a charismatic African American activist in an era of racial strife.

King, Greg
The Mad King: A Biography of Ludwig II of Bavaria. 1996. Birch Lane Press. 335p. ISBN 1559723629.

With good intentions and much reluctance, Ludwig II of Bavaria (1845–1886) became king of Germany at 18. Always shy, he quickly grew to hate his duties in Munich and fled to the countryside, where he built castles and enjoyed private performances of grand opera. Days after being deposed at 41, he was found floating dead in a lake. Historical biographer Greg King recounts the life of a king who let his country fall under the control of ambitious and malicious men who paved the path to world war.

McQuillar, Tayannah Lee, and Fred L. Johnson III
Tupac Shakur: The Life and Times of an American Icon. 2010. Dacapo Press. 276p. ISBN 8671568583877.

Rapper Tupac Shakur (1971–1996) was born into a culture of poverty and radical protest. His mother had been in the Weather Underground and never provided a stable home. He attended an elite high school for the arts and, for a brief time, was poised to escape from the ghetto. He used new-found eloquence to become a musical star, but he lacked street smarts to escape drugs and violence. In this sympathetic biography, rap historian Tayannah Lee Mc-Quillar and cultural historian Fred L. Johnson III recount the difficult life of a young man who ultimately lacked the will to succeed.

Pringle, Peter
The Murder of Nikolai Vavilov: The Story of Stalin's Persecution of One of the Great Scientists of the Twentieth Century. 2008. Simon & Schuster. 368p. ISBN 9780743264983.

 The Soviet years were a dark time for Russian scientists. While most of them fled to the West during the Bolshevik Revolution, plant geneticist Nikolai Vavilov (1887–1943) stayed to work for Vladimir Lenin's agricultural initiative, eventually becoming director of the Bureau of Applied Botany. In this sympathetic biography, Peter Pringle tells how Joseph Stalin's collectivization of farms sabotaged Vavilov's work to improve Russian crops, but Vavilov was blamed for the resulting famines and was sent to prison where he starved to death.

Stenn, David
Bombshell: The Life and Death of Jean Harlow. 1993. Doubleday. 370p. ISBN 0385421575.

 The death of actress Jean Harlow (1911–1937) from liver failure at 26 was the final tragedy in a life that could have been delightful. Being a rich girl from Kansas City and then a tremendously successful actress at MGM Studios, Harlow seemed to be a young star with limitless possibilities. But, behind the glamour of her life was discord and addiction. Investigative author David Stenn reveals the fragile actress torn by a dysfunctional family in this sympathetic biography.

Psychological Depths

 A primary reason for reading biographies is to gain deeper understanding of a person's life (and maybe one's own), but psychological depictions have not always been considered ethical. Through the 19th century, biographers were charged with simply presenting the facts to tell what their subjects had accomplished. Until Sigmund Freud's publication of psychological case studies, biographers mostly avoided writing about their subjects' deep and sometimes unspoken motivations. Now, psychological speculation is a common element in biography. The following titles are psychologically intense accounts of troubled characters.

Carlin, Peter Ames
Catch a Wave: The Rise, Fall and Redemption of the Beach Boy's Brian Wilson. 2006. Rodale. 342p. ISBN 9781594863202.

 While recording an album for Capitol Records in 1969, Brian Wilson (1942–) proposed the Beach Boys change the band's juvenile name, but no one else would consider his proposal. The gulf between Wilson and the rest of the world was widening. Musical disagreements, use of drugs, and escaping the intense expectations of his father tormented him constantly. Then, he cracked. Author Peter Ames Carlin pieces together stories from Wilson's life, from early childhood to the release of the long-lost album *Smile* in 2005, in this deeply analytical biography.

Colapinto, John

As Nature Made Him: The Boy Who Was Raised as a Girl. 2000. HarperCollins. 278p. ISBN 0060192119. ☙

Is sexual identity taught or is it instinctive? In the 1960s, medical journals prematurely reported that an anonymous boy was successfully being raised as a girl after his penis had been damaged and removed during a botched circumcision. Journalist John Colapinto thoughtfully recounts how determined psychologists, with the help of his parents, tried to deceive young David Reimer (1965–2004), a man who struggled with his self-image.

Nielsen, Kim E.

Beyond the Miracle Worker: The Remarkable Life of Anne Sullivan Macy and Her Extraordinary Friendship with Helen Keller. 2009. Beacon Press. 299p. ISBN 9780807050460.

In the story of Helen Keller overcoming deafness and blindness to become an internationally known author and humanitarian, Anne Sullivan Macy (1866–1936) is seen as an important but secondary character. While Macy's loyalty and determination are recognized, her motivations are usually not examined. Few readers know the abject poverty from which she rose and how she came to rely on Keller's close friendship to stave off depression. Keller scholar Kim E. Nielsen intimately recounts Macy's struggles in this psychological biography.

Pizzichini, Lilian

Blue Hour: A Life of Jean Rhys. 2009. W. W. Norton. 322p. ISBN 9780393058031.

From numerous crossings of the Atlantic Ocean, leaving and returning to her birthplace in the West Indies, British novelist Jean Rhys (1890–1979) knew well the Sargasso Sea, the seemingly calm waters that can be difficult to escape. With each trip, she embarked on another phase of her life, trying to leave behind pain and insecurity, sometimes failing miserably. Biographer Lilian Pizzichini recounts the emotion-filled life of a woman who found beauty and talent insufficient.

Prideaux, Sue

Edvard Munch: Behind the Scream. 2005. Yale University Press. 391p. ISBN 0300110243.

Norwegian artist Edvard Munch (1863–1944) said that his paintings and drawings of a suicidal lover, mentally ill sister, and himself formed a diary of his soul. Using rounded figures floating among swirling colors, he repeatedly turned to the themes of insecurity, terror, and grief. In this attractive psychological biography that contains numerous color plates, art historian Sue Prideaux sorts through Munch's confusing portfolio to create an understandable narrative of the tormented artist.

Rose, Phyllis
Jazz Cleopatra: Josephine Baker in Her Time. 1989. Doubleday. 321p. ISBN 0385248911.

"J'ai deux amours," sang Josephine Baker (1906–1975), who loved Paris so much that she became a French citizen and served in the resistance during World War II. American audiences had never embraced the African American singer as had the French. As a child in St. Louis, she was abandoned by her parents to be raised by relatives. Then, though a very talented jazz dancer, she was just one of many entertainers in New York. In France, she became a star and adopted a dozen children. Author Phyllis Rose speculates on Baker's emotional needs in this psychologically focused account.

Weissman, Stephen M.
▶ *Chaplin: A Life*. 2008. Arcade. 315p. ISBN 9781559708920.

Charlie Chaplin (1889–1977) entered the Hanwell School for Orphans and Destitute Children in London at seven when his mother could no longer support her children by singing in music halls or with sweatshop piecework. His alcoholic father, also a music hall singer, had already abandoned them. Chaplin's life quickly fell from being a child dressed in velvet to being a ward of the state. Psychiatrist Stephen M. Weissman weaves an account of Chaplin's Dickensesque early years with an examination of his surprisingly autobiographical films in this unapologetically psychological biography.

Heartwarming Stories

In times when newspapers and television are filled with bad news and discord, many people long to find sweet positive stories without violence, graphic sex, and rough language. Librarians sometimes call such books gentle reads. The following biographies will appeal to such readers who request books that fondly describe the lives of admirable people, such as Audrey Hepburn, E.B. White, and Emma Darwin.

Brinkley, Douglas, and Julie M. Fenster
Parish Priest: Father Michael McGivney and American Catholicism. 2006. William Morrow. 240p. ISBN 9780060776848.

Roman Catholic priest Michael McGivney (1852–1890) spent nearly his entire life in Connecticut, first as the child of a foundry worker in Waterbury and later as a priest in several parishes. His reputation as a champion of the poor, however, spread around the world through his work with the Knights of Columbus, a fraternal organization he founded in 1882. In this tribute to a candidate for sainthood, authors Douglas Brinkley and Julie M. Fenster recount the compassionate life of a simple parish priest who helped Irish Catholics at a time when they were loathed by other Americans.

Dennison, Matthew
***The Last Princess: The Devoted Life of Queen Victoria's Youngest Daughter*.** 2008. St. Martin's Press. 302p. ISBN 9780312376987.

As the ninth and last child of the extremely domineering Queen Victoria of Great Britain, Princess Beatrice (1857–1944) was the most available companion for her mother after the death of her father Prince Albert in 1861. Having already proved to be a happy child who elicited previously absent maternal feelings from the queen, Beatrice bloomed in the role and succeeded in circumventing her mother's objections to her finding a husband. With this admittedly sympathetic biography, journalist Matthew Dennison reminds modern readers of a time when royalty was venerated by loyal subjects.

Elledge, Scott
▶ ***E. B. White: A Biography*.** 1984. W. W. Norton. 400p. ISBN 0393017710.

While older readers may associate author E. B. White (1899–1985) with his literary pieces in the *New Yorker*, younger readers think of his classic children's books *Charlotte's Web* and *Stuart Little*. His light touch at all levels of writing won him the affection of many fans. In this admiring biography, Scott Elledge recounts the life of a funny and gentle man with many remarkable friends and a long happy marriage.

Feinstein, John
***Caddy for Life: The Bruce Edwards Story*.** 2004. Little Brown. 300p. ISBN 031677889.

Many successful golfers have devoted caddies who partner with them through their careers. One such caddy was Bruce Edwards (1954–2004) who worked for more than 20 years with pro golfer Tom Watson. At Edwards's request, sportswriter John Feinstein shadowed the caddy through the last year of his life as he fought amyotrophic lateral sclerosis (ALS), known as Lou Gehrig's disease. Readers do not have to be sports fans to be touched by this admiring account of Edwards's emotional farewell tour.

Ferrer, Sean Hepburn
***Audrey Hepburn, an Elegant Spirit*.** 2003. Atria Books. 230p. ISBN 0671024787.

To author Sean Hepburn Ferrer, actress Audrey Hepburn (1929–1993) was not just a famous person—she was his mother. As you might expect, this son's biography of his mother is kind, but in this case, it is also convincing. Along with stories about Hepburn's devotion to her children and many friendships are accounts of her charity work for children around the world. Hepburn fans will especially enjoy the many family photographs.

Loy, James D., and Kent M. Loy
Emma Darwin: A Victorian Life. 2010. University of Florida Press. 436p. ISBN 9780813034782.

> *Loyal* and *devoted* are the words most often used to describe Emma Wedgwood Darwin (1808–1896), wife of British naturalist Charles Darwin. Authors James D. Loy and Kent M. Loy add "intelligent, educated, and religious." In their admiring biography drawn heavily from Emma's letters to her husband and family, they describe her as a remarkable partner who edited her husband's papers and respectfully questioned his ideas, even when she found them challenging her own beliefs. She also entertained his guests, ran his house, raised his children, and nursed him through many illnesses. The Loys offer her as a model of tolerance often missing in today's world.

Miller, Marla R.
Betsy Ross and the Making of America. 2010. Henry Holt. 467p. ISBN 9780805082975. ⮑

> The oft-repeated story is that George Washington personally asked Philadelphia seamstress Betsy Ross (1752–1836) to make the first flag for the newly declared nation. Ross herself told the undocumented story many times. In this admiring biography of the revolutionary heroine, historian Marla R. Miller argues that Ross led a remarkable life regardless of whether the flag story is true. Miller recounts the life of an industrious woman known for her upholstery and flags, who worked for more than 50 years, survived three husbands, and raised seven daughters while supporting her community and country.

Waldron, Daniel
Blackstone, A Magician's Life: The World and Magic Show of Harry Blackstone, 1885–1965. 1999. David Meyer/Magic Books. 230p. ISBN 091663891x.

> Harry Boughton (1885–1965) wanted a glamorous life. He was just a teenager working in a machine shop in Chicago when he began performing magic tricks for his mother's social club. Inspired by vaudeville magic acts that played in the city, he studied many tricks at the local Roterberg Magic Shop. Author Daniel Waldron lovingly tells how a Midwestern boy transformed himself into the sophisticated and world-famous Harry Blackstone, an extraordinary magician who sawed pretty ladies in half and raised his son to do the same.

Pure Nostalgia

Fans of celebrities are often fans for life. They enjoy reading everything that they can find about their favorite subjects and prefer light-hearted, picture-filled accounts. They will accept some acknowledgements of their idols' faults so long as the books are generally sympathetic. Fan books about Elvis Presley, Walt Disney, and other famous figures return the readers to bygone times when they had fewer cares and more enthusiasm for music, movies, and sports.

Chandler, Charlotte
Ingrid: Ingrid Bergman, a Personal Biography. 2007. Simon & Schuster. 334p. ISBN 9780743294218, 0743294211.

> So many quotes from actress Ingrid Bergman (1915–1982) are used in this quick read that it seems almost a memoir. The author often says, "Ingrid told me." She also quotes many great directors, including George Cukor, Federico Fellini, Alfred Hitchcock, and Roberto Rossellini, and includes passages from Bergman's daughter Isabella. At appropriate points, she inserts movie-plot summaries, making the book a great read for film fans.

Chierichetti, David
▶ *Edith Head: The Life and Times of Hollywood's Celebrated Costume Designer*. 2003. HarperCollins. 251p. ISBN 0060194286.

> Winner of 10 Academy Awards for best costume design, Edith Head (1897–1981) worked with all of the top actors and actresses during Hollywood's most glamorous years. Seen often on television from the 1950s to the 1970s, the woman behind the big glasses became almost as famous as the leading ladies she dressed. Through stories and photos, film historian David Chierichetti recalls the fun of watching classic movies in which the stars were glamorously dressed.

George-Warren, Holly
Public Cowboy No. 1: The Life and Times of Gene Autry. 2007. Oxford University Press. 406p. ISBN 9780195177466.

> From the late 1920s into the 1950s, America's most loved singing cowboy was Gene Autry (1907–1998). While selling over 100 million recordings of songs, such as "Back in the Saddle Again" and "Rudolph the Red-Nosed Reindeer," Autry played cowboys on radio, in the movies, and on television. A generation grew up seeing the happy cowboy at movie matinees and on tour with his own rodeo. In this detailed account of the singer's life, music critic Holly George-Warren reveals that Autry always had a keen eye for business as well as an ability to charm the public with his mythical vision of the American West.

Green, Amy Boothe, and Howard E. Green
Remembering Walt: Favorite Memories of Walt Disney. 1999. Hyperion. 212p. ISBN 078686348X.

> Baby boomers fondly remember animator, movie producer, and theme park mogul Walt Disney (1901–1966) as Uncle Walt. He was the adult who seemed to be most like them, always seeking fun. According to veteran Disney employees Amy Boothe Green and Howard E. Green, Disney was just as warm

in person as on television. They weave together stories from family, friends, employees, and the stars of Disney movies in this lighthearted tribute.

Louvish, Simon
Stan and Ollie: The Roots of Comedy: The Double Life of Laurel and Hardy. 2002. Thomas Dunne Books. 520p. ISBN 0312266510.

Comedians Oliver Hardy (1892–1957) and Stan Laurel (1890–1965) rose from the dog-eat-dog world of minstrel shows and vaudeville to become stars of both silent and early sound films. Audiences worldwide laughed at their slapstick antics. The bedlam of their on-screen lives spilled into their personal lives, as both struggled with money and marriages. In this sympathetic dual biography, novelist Simon Louvish recounts comic dialogues that can still make readers laugh.

Mason, Bobbie Ann
Elvis Presley. **Penguin Lives**. 2003. Lipper/Viking. 178p. ISBN 0670031747. ≋

Besides being a respected novelist, Bobbie Ann Mason is a lifelong fan of Elvis Presley (1935–1977). She followed closely as he recorded hit records, appeared on national television shows, made movies, went into the army, met the Beatles, headlined Las Vegas casino shows, and then died prematurely. In this volume from the acclaimed Penguin Lives series of compact biographies, she recounts why Presley's music and movie career meant so much to his fans.

Smith, Curt
Pull Up a Chair: The Vin Scully Story. 2009. Potomac Books. 264p. ISBN 9781597974240.

Silver-tongued Los Angeles Dodgers broadcaster Vin Scully (1927–) has witnessed more than 60 years of baseball history. As a play-by-play announcer, he called four Sandy Koufax no-hitters, Hank Aaron breaking Babe Ruth's career home run record, and Jackie Robinson leading his team to the World Series. Scully has also worked with all the most famous radio and television sportscasters, including Red Barber, Mel Allen, Joe Garagiola, and Bob Costas. Sports historian Curt Smith recounts Scully's celebrated career in this admiring biography.

Zehme, Bill
The Way You Wear Your Hat: Frank Sinatra and the Lost Art of Livin'. 1997. HarperCollins. 245p. ISBN 006018289X.

Looking good was as important to singer and actor Frank Sinatra (1915–1998) as singing in tune. The so-called Chairman of the Board also wanted all his friends to follow his example. Admiring author Bill Zehme describes the Sinatra style and recommended behaviors in this collection of lighthearted biographical essays on clothes, friends, families, women, and performing.

Glorious Gossip

One negative view of biographers is that they are muckrakers, opportunists who recycle rumor and scandal for their own fame and fortune. They specialize in telling unsavory stories that feature infidelity, illegitimacy, and ill-gotten gains. Of course, there may also be truth behind the gossip about celebrities, such as former Beatle Paul McCartney, sex scientists Masters and Johnson, and television mogul Oprah Winfrey. Readers may have much fun trying to decide for themselves the merits of the following stories.

Carlin, Peter Ames
Paul McCartney: A Life. 2009. Simon & Schuster. 374p. ISBN 781416562092.
    John Lennon had no idea what impact inviting Paul McCartney (1942–) to join The Quarrymen would have on his life. Ambitious and mischievous, McCartney hijacked Lennon's skiffle band, propelling the duo and their new mates into the raucous world of sex, drugs, and rock and roll. Former *People* magazine writer Peter Ames Carlin breezily recounts McCartney's music and personal relationships in this story of a poor Liverpool boy made rich and famous.

Edwards, Anne
Maria Callas: An Intimate Biography. 2001. St. Martin's Press. 342p. ISBN 0312269862.
    Anne Edwards is known for her tattle-filled biographies of celebrities from the arts and politics. In this classic example of her work, Edwards focuses on the career and off-stage relationships of stormy opera diva Maria Callas (1923–1977). Partly an ugly-duckling-turns-swan story with large doses of ambition, greed, and jealousy, this biography offers stories about high art, high society, and a woman who died tragically young.

Halperin, Ian
Brangelina: The Untold Story of Brad Pitt and Angelina Jolie. 2009. Transit. 271p. ISBN 9780981239668.
    For this chronicle of Brad Pitt (1963–) and Angelina Jolie (1975–), pop biographer Ian Halperin infiltrated a psychiatric hospital, the 72-hour home of Jolie just before she became an internationally famous movie star. Halperin emerged from reading the private files impressed by Jolie's ability to reinvent her persona, but he was also concerned that she had set too high a goal for life. Where does Brad Pitt fit into the actress's plan? Halperin reports his findings in this intimate biography.

Kelley, Kitty
Oprah: A Biography. 2010. Crown Publishers. 524p. ISBN 9780307394866. ☃
    For nearly three decades, television talk show host Oprah Winfrey (1954–) has pried secrets out of the legions of guests who have appeared on her

nationally syndicated program. Both celebrities and everyday people have described abuse, addiction, obsession, and other unpleasant details of their lives. At what unauthorized biographer Kitty Kelley typifies as calculated moments, Winfrey has dramatically revealed selected traumas from her own life and captured the attention of millions of television viewers. Weighing the good and the bad, Kelley recounts what she has discovered (with no help from the subject) about America's most powerful woman.

Maier, Thomas
Masters of Sex: The Life and Times of William Masters and Virginia Johnson, the Couple Who Taught America How to Love. 2009. Basic Books. 411p. ISBN 9780465003075.

During their careers as researchers, William Masters (1915–2001) and Virginia Johnson (1925–) kept much about their work and their lives secret. Being academics and respecting the privacy of their volunteers for sex research made discretion essential. They also had marriages to protect. Having interviewed the couple and read Masters's autobiographical manuscript, investigative reporter Thomas Maier methodically recounts how Masters and Johnson were unable to stay professionally aloof amidst the passions in their laboratory.

Mann, William J.
▶ *How to Be a Movie Star: Elizabeth Taylor in Hollywood*. 2009. Houghton Mifflin. 484p. ISBN 9780547134642. 🐚

Long before our current wave of beautiful people mined the celebrity press and Internet for publicity, actress Elizabeth Taylor (1932–2011) mastered the system. Though her every move was followed by the paparazzi, she was not its victim. Celebrity biographer William J. Mann drew from interviews with previously reluctant sources to write this juicy story about a beautiful and talented woman in control of her career.

Redfern, Nick
Celebrity Secrets: Government Files on the Rich and Famous. 2007. Paraview Pocket Books. 252p. ISBN 9781416528661.

The Federal Bureau of Investigation, the Central Intelligence Agency, and the various branches of U.S. military intelligence always assume the worst, according to journalist Nick Redfern, who has read the agencies' declassified files on celebrities. In this entertaining collective biography, he reports on the secret profiles of actors, comedians, singers, and other entertainers suspected of criminal activity. To their credit, the law agencies found some disturbing evidence and rejected some obviously ridiculous reports, but they also used illegal surveillance methods and pursued lines of inquiry long after it was clear that there was nothing to find. Abbot and Costello, Marilyn Monroe, Frank Sinatra, Sonny Bono, and John Lennon were all suspects.

Schnakenberg, Heidi

Kid Carolina: R. J. Reynolds Jr., a Tobacco Fortune, and the Mysterious Death of a Southern Icon. 2010. Center Street. 332p. ISBN 9781599951034.

Sons of tycoons are often overshadowed in life and in history. R.J. Reynolds Jr. (1906–1964) was no exception. His role in expanding the family tobacco company and in forming the Eastern and Delta Airlines partnership were not publicized in his time, but his divorces, auto accidents, and opulent lifestyle were society page news. Using imagined conversations, screenwriter Heidi Schnakenberg recounts the indulgent life of the mid-20th-century millionaire.

Thurman, Judith

Secrets of the Flesh: A Life of Colette. 1999. Alfred A. Knopf. 592p. ISBN 039458872X.

As author of the fictional diary *Claudine at School*, French novelist Colette (1873–1954) remained anonymous, an ironic beginning to the literary career of one of France's most famous libertines. All of France would soon know of her marriages and many affairs, see her half-dressed on the Paris stage, and read her many stories, memoirs, and plays. Though Colette's every thought and action seemed for a time public, biographer Judith Thurman contends that the novelist kept her true character hidden behind contradictions.

Author-Title Index

141

Subject Index

157

About the Author

RICK ROCHE is head of the Adult Services Department at the Thomas Ford Memorial Library in Western Springs, Illinois. A graduate of the Graduate School of Library and Information Science at the University of Texas at Austin, he has worked at libraries in Texas, Missouri, and Illinois. He is the author of *Real Lives Revealed: A Guide to Reading Interests in Biography*, reviews science books for *Booklist*, and comments on books, movies, and technology at libraries at his website, ricklibrarian.blogspot.com.

Edwards Brothers Malloy
Thorofare, NJ USA
August 28, 2012